Thank you for returning
your books on time.

Abington Free Library
1030 Old York Road
Abington, PA 19001

Like a Rolling Stone

Also by Greil Marcus

Mystery Train: Images of America in Rock 'n' Roll Music (1975)

Lipstick Traces: A Secret History of the 20th Century (1989)

Dead Elvis: A Chronicle of a Cultural Obsession (1991)

In the Fascist Bathroom: Punk in Pop Music, 1977–92 (1993, originally published as *Ranters & Crowd Pleasers*)

The Dustbin of History (1995)

The Old, Weird America: The World of Bob Dylan's Basement Tapes (1997, originally published as *Invisible Republic*)

Double Trouble: Bill Clinton and Elvis Presley in a Land of No Alternatives (2000)

"The Manchurian Candidate" (2002)

AS EDITOR:

Stranded (1979)

Psychotic Reactions & Carburetor Dung, by Lester Bangs (1987)

The Rose & the Briar: Death, Love and Liberty in the American Ballad (2004, with Sean Wilentz)

LIKE A ROLLING STONE

Bob Dylan at the Crossroads

GREIL MARCUS

PublicAffairs

New York

Published in the United States by PublicAffairs™,
a member of the Perseus Books Group.

Book design by Mark McGarry
Set in Weiss

Library of Congress Cataloging-in-Publication data
Marcus, Greil.
Like a Rolling Stone / Bob Dylan at the Crossroads.—1st ed.
p. cm.
Includes bibliographical references and index.
ISBN 1–58648–254–8 (HB)
1. Dylan, Bob, 1941—Like a Rolling Stone. I. Title
ML420.D98M163 2005
782.42164 2004058583—dc22
2004060053

FIRST EDITION
10 9 8 7 6 5 4 3 2 1

To the radio

Like a Rolling Stone

Once upon a time you dressed so fine
Threw the bums a dime, in your prime
Didn't you?
People call, say beware doll, you're bound to fall, you
    thought they were all
A-kiddin' you
You used to
Laugh about
Everybody that was
Hangin' out
Now you don't
Talk so loud
Now you don't
Seem so proud
About havin' to be scrounging
Your next meal

    How does it feel?
    How does it feel

To be without a home
Like a complete unknown
Like a rolling stone?

Aw you've
Gone to the finest school alright Miss Lonely but you know
      you only used to get
Juiced in it
Nobody's ever taught you how to live out on the street
And now you're gonna
Have to get
Used to it
You say you never
Compromise
With the mystery tramp but now you
Realize
He's not selling any
Alibis
As you stare into the vacuum
Of his eyes
And say
Do you want to
Make a deal?

How does it feel?
How does it feel?
To be on your own

With no direction home
A complete unknown
Like a rolling stone

Ah, you
Never turned around to see the frowns
On the jugglers and the clowns when they all did
Tricks for you
Never understood that it ain't no good
You shouldn't
Let other people
Get your
Kicks for you
You used to ride on a chrome horse with your
Diplomat
Who carried on his shoulder a
Siamese cat
Ain't it hard
When you discover that
He really wasn't
Where it's at
After he took from you everything
He could steal?

How does it feel?
How does it feel
To have you on your own

No direction home
Like a complete unknown
Like a rolling stone

Ahhhhhhhh—
Princess on the steeple and all the
Pretty people they're all drinkin' thinkin' that they
Got it made
Exchanging all precious gifts
But you better
Take your diamond ring
You better pawn it, babe
You used to be
So amused
At Napoleon in rags
And the language that he used
Go to him now, he calls you, you can't refuse
When you ain't got nothin'
You got
Nothing to lose
You're invisible now, you got no secrets
To conceal

How does it feel
Ah, how does it feel
To be on your own
With no direction

As sung by Bob Dylan, New York City, 16 June 1965. Six minutes and six seconds. Produced by Tom Wilson. Engineered by Roy Halee, with Pete Duryea, assistant engineer. Michael Bloomfield, guitar; Bob Dylan, rhythm guitar and harmonica; Bobby Gregg, drums; Paul Griffin, piano; Al Kooper, organ; Bruce Langhorne, tambourine; Joe Macho, Jr., bass guitar. Released as Columbia 45 43346 on July 20. First entered *Billboard* Hot 100 July 24. Highest chart position reached: number 2, September 4. Number one that week: the Beatles, "Help."

CONTENTS

Contents

When I died, love, when I died
there was a war in the upper air;
All that happens, happens there

—Allen Ginsberg,
"A Western Ballad," 1948

This and the following photographs from the first day of
sessions for "Like a Rolling Stone," 15 June 1965, taken
by Don Hunstein, Columbia Records. Here: Bob Dylan
at the piano, with lyrics, page after page.

Prologue

In Columbia Records Studio A on 15 June 1965, the singer is trying to find his way into his song, plinking notes on the piano. There's a feeling of uplift, dashed as soon as he begins to sing. His voice sounds as if it's just come back from the dry cleaners three sizes too small. He forces a few random notes out of his harmonica. The 3/4 beat is painful, weighing down the already sway-backed melody until it falls flat on the ground. The organist pushes his way into the music, like a bystander at an accident determined to do something to help, no matter how hopeless: *Are you all right?* The tune dries up after a minute and a half. "The voice is gone, man," the singer says. "You want to try it again?"

"It's a waltz, man," says the producer.

"It's not a waltz," the singer says.

"May I have this dance?"

"Have you heard about the new Bob Dylan record?"

"No, what about it?"

"It's called 'Like a Rolling Stone.' Can you believe that? Like a *Rolling Stone*. Like he wants to join the band. Like *he's* a Rolling Stone."

"What does it sound like?"

"I don't know. It's not out yet. I read about it."

"You're kidding, right?"

"So who's the 'Napoleon in rags' the girl in the song used to laugh at? The music is great, the words are a bunch of nonsense."

"It's obviously Dylan himself. 'The language that he used.' It's like he's putting down someone who didn't like his songs."

"He's not that stupid. That can't be it."

"Yeah, so who is it if it's not him?"

"I don't know. Martin Luther King?"

Questioner: "What happens if they have to cut a song in half like 'Subterranean Homesick Blues'?"

Bob Dylan: "They didn't have to cut that in half."

"They didn't have to but they did."

"No, they didn't."

"Yeah?"

"You're talking about 'Like a Rolling Stone.'"

"Oh, yeah."

"They cut it in half for the disc jockeys. Well, you see, it didn't matter for the disc jockeys if they had it cut in half, because the other side was just a continuation . . . if anybody was interested they could just turn it over and listen to what really happens."

— press conference, San Francisco, 3 December 1965

A drum beat like a pistol shot.

24 July 1965 was the day Bob Dylan's "Like a Rolling Stone" went into the charts. It was on the radio all across the U.S.A. and heading straight up. When drummer Bobby Gregg brought his stick down for the opening noise of the six-minute single, the sound—a kind of announcement, then a void of silence, then a rising fanfare, then the song—fixed a moment when all those caught up in modern music found themselves engaged in a running battle for a prize no one bothered to name: the greatest record ever made, perhaps, or the greatest record that ever would be made. "Where are we going? To the top?" the Beatles would ask themselves in the early 1960s, when no one but they knew. "To the toppermost of the poppermost!" they promised themselves, even before their manager Brian Epstein began writing London record companies on his provincial Liverpool stationary, promising that his new group would someday be bigger than Elvis. But by 1965 everyone, the Beatles, the Rolling Stones, Bob

Dylan, and whoever else could catch a ride on the train were topping each other month by month, as if carried by a flood. Was it the flood of fear and possibility that had convulsed much of the West since the assassination of President Kennedy less than two years before, a kind of nihilist freedom, in which old certainties were swept away like trees and cars? The utopian revolt of the Civil Rights Movement, or the strange cultures appearing in college towns and cities across the nation, in England, in Germany? No one heard the music on the radio as part of a separate reality. Every new hit seemed full of novelty, as if its goal was not only to top the charts but to stop the world in its tracks and then start it up again. What was the top? Fame and fortune, glamour and style, or something else? A sound that you could leave behind, to mark your presence on the earth, something that would circulate in the ether of lost radio signals, somehow received by generations to come, or apprehended even by those who were already gone? The chance to make the times speak in your own voice, or the chance to discover the voice of the times?

Early in the year the Beatles had kicked off the race with the shimmering thrill of the opening and closing chords of "Eight Days a Week." No one could imagine a more joyous sound. In March the Rolling Stones put out the deathly, oddly quiet "Play with Fire," a single that seemed to call the whole pop equation of happiness, speed, and excitement into question: to undercut it with a refusal to be ashamed of one's own intelligence, to suspend the contest in a cul-de-sac of doubt. Three months later they came back with "(I Can't Get No) Satisfaction." It erased the doubt, and the race was on again.

Bob Dylan had not really come close with "Subterranean Homesick Blues" in April, his first rock 'n' roll record after four albums—four folk albums that had nevertheless redrawn the pop map—and his first entry into the singles charts. The Beatles would dominate the second half of the year with "Yesterday" (was a record with nothing but strings still rock 'n' roll? "Of course it is," said a friend. "John Lennon has to be playing one of the violins"), and end it with the coolly subtle *Rubber Soul*, the best album they would ever make. Barry McGuire would reach number one with "Eve of Destruction," an imitation-Dylan big-beat protest song. The Dylan imitation was the hook, what grabbed you—and the production was so formulaic, so plainly a jump on a trend, that the formula and the trend became hooks in themselves. In that season, to hear "Eve of Destruction" as a fake was also to recognize that the world behind it, a world of racism, war, greed, starvation, and lies, was real—and, as if apocalypse was itself just another hook, actually deserved to be destroyed. In the pop arena it seemed anything could happen; it seemed that month by month everything did. The race was not only between the Beatles, Bob Dylan, the Rolling Stones, and everyone else. The pop world was in a race with the greater world, the world of wars and elections, work and leisure, poverty and riches, white people and black people, women and men—and in 1965 you could feel that the pop world was winning.

When people first heard about it, even before they first heard it, "Like a Rolling Stone" seemed less like a piece of music than a stroke of upsmanship beyond pop ken. "Eight of the Top Ten songs were Beatles songs," Bob Dylan would remember years later, casting back to a day in Colorado, listening to John, Paul, George, and Ringo soon after their arrival in the United States in 1964. "I knew they were pointing the direction where music had to go ... It seemed to me a definite line was being drawn. This was something that had never happened before." That was the moment that took Bob Dylan out of his folk singer's clothes—and now here he was, outflanking the Rolling Stones with a song *about* them. That was the word.

The pop moment, in that season, really was that delirious. But when the song hit the radio, when people heard it, when they discovered that it wasn't about a band, they realized that the song did not explain itself at all, and that they didn't care. In the wash of words and instruments, people understood that the song was a rewrite of the world itself. An old world was facing a dare it wasn't ready for; as the song traced its long arc across the radio, a world that was taking shape seemed altogether in flux. As the composer Michael Pisaro wrote in 2004, "Like a Rolling Stone" might be "a song that has as its backdrop some problems the guy narrating it is having with his girl." It might be even more, a warning to someone for whom everything has always come easily, in times that are about to get rough, "but I am unable to hear it so simply: that is, that he (or the world) has done her the favor of stripping away her illusions, and now she can live honestly." Pisaro goes on, in a few words that are like a launching pad:

His conviction, the dead certainty that he has a right to say exactly this, is still exhilarating and bone-chilling. After all these years the song has not been dulled by time and repetition.

In some ways it's also a difficult song to hear now, because it is a vision of a time that never came to pass. I may be wrong about this, since I was only four years old in 1965. But that time (or is it the time *created* by the song?) seems to have been the last moment in American history when the country might have changed, in a fundamental way, for the better. The song, even now, registers this possibility, brings it to a point, focuses your attention on it, and then forces you to decide what is to be done.

His voice tells you this (tells you everything): he's not really talking to her—he's talking to *you* (and me; all of us). The voice is infinitely nuanced—at times an almost authoritarian monotone (not unlike Ginsberg reading "Howl"), at times compassionate, tragic (the voice of Jacques-Louis David in his painting of Marat)—but also angry, vengeful, gleeful, ironic, weary, spectral, haranguing. And it would sound this way in Ancient Greek or contemporary Russian. There is so much desire and so much power in this voice, translated into a sensitivity that enables it to detect tiny vibrations emanating from the earth. But like a Geiger counter developing a will of its own, it wavers between trying to record the coming quake and trying to *make it happen*. This is where the song stakes its claim on eternity.

And then Pisaro is in the air, looking down as the song continues to play and the landscape begins to convulse:

What is the nature of the decision Dylan is driving towards? Whether you are going to forsake your past in the name of an unknowable future, where nothing is certain, everything is up for grabs, no food, no home, just a wagon barreling down the road. It is not a sensible decision. Of course some at the time made exactly this decision, but what strikes me about Dylan's song is that he's not only asking you (and me) personally to make this decision, he wants the whole country to do it: *right now*. As if a country could shed its past like snakeskin. As if, if we could see our situation with clarity, we would realize we are already there. I have to hear this as a call for some kind of spontaneous revolution. Not necessarily a violent one; but undoubtedly a very *strange* one. What would a "Napoleon in rags" kind of country look like, act like? Lots of poor folks wandering the land, making speeches and barbeque?

Or, as reviewer Shirley Poston put it in *The Beat*, the newsletter of the Los Angeles Top 40 station KRLA, after

Dylan's performance of "Like a Rolling Stone" at the Holly-wood Bowl on 3 September 1965, only the third time he had played the song in public, with the tune still finding its feet, and with some in the crowd booing the once-humble folk singer who had gone for the pop charts: "He knew the song by heart. So did his audience."

People then understood everything Pisaro is saying now. But then the sense of moment ruled. Few had any reason to imagine that in "Like a Rolling Stone" the pull of the past was as strong as the pull of the future—and the pull of the future, the future that first drum shot was announcing, the line it was drawing, was very strong. There was no reason to wonder how many dead or vanished voices the song contained, or to realize that along with the song's own named characters—"Miss Lonely," the "Mystery Tramp," the "Diplomat"—or Phil Spector and the Righteous Brothers' "You've Lost that Lovin' Feeling," from only months before, or even Ritchie Valens's "La Bamba," from 1958—present also were the likes of Son House, of Mississippi, with "My Black Mama" from 1930, Hank Williams with "Lost Highway" from 1949, or Muddy Waters in 1950, with "Rollin' Stone." So the Rolling Stones had named themselves—in the beginning, in London in 1962, they were the Rollin' Stones. Which is to say that in the alchemy of pop the first word about "Like a Rolling Stone" had been right after all. The song was about the

Rolling Stones—if you follow the way the two words travel and the picture they make, how nothing in American vernacular music holds still, how every phrase and image, every riff and chime, is always moving, state to state, decade to decade, never at home with whoever might claim it, always seeking a new body, a new song, a new voice.

PART ONE

CHAPTER ONE

The Day Kennedy Was Shot

"Everyone remembers where they were when they heard that Kennedy was shot. I wonder how many people remember where they were when they first heard Bob Dylan's voice. It's so *unexpected*." So said a friend a year or two ago; I started thinking about how the world still seemed to be catching up with Dylan's *Time Out of Mind*, which had appeared in 1997—or how the world might even be falling behind it. Maybe even Dylan himself, with his *"Love and Theft"* in 2001. It was a collection of songs so well-shaped that up against the scattered American nowheres of *Time Out of Mind*—with various places named, Missouri, say, Chicago, Boston, New Orleans, but all of them still floating free of any map, with the music so ragged it seemed a new black hole opened up even before you cleared the one before it—*"Love and Theft"* could feel like a step back. A step off the battlefield, a step off the train.

I remember very clearly where I was the first time I heard Bob Dylan's voice. It was in 1963, in early August, in a field in southern New Jersey. I was spending the summer in Philadelphia; I'd gone to see Joan Baez, a familiar face in Menlo Park, California, my home town. The year before, I'd crossed the street between my parents' house and the Quaker school where I'd taken writing classes from Baez's mentor Ira Sandperl to find Baez and her sister Mimi entertaining a circle of little kids with a version of the Marvelettes' "Playboy."

Mimi Baez was so pretty it was hard to look at her. Joan Baez was hard to look at, too—because already, even in the most casual setting, she could appear less as a person than a myth. It was the music she wrapped around herself like wings, like a shroud—a sense of the departed, the untouchable, the never-was brought forward as if it were the soon-to-be—that removed her from the noise of the country at large. Her music removed her from that noise even as she added her voice to it, to the chorus of all those now calling for the destruction of nuclear weapons, for the abolition of racial segregation—all those calling, as Martin Luther King would prophesy before the Lincoln Memorial in Washington, D.C., only weeks after that day in the New Jersey field, ringing his words like bells as Joan Baez like Bob Dylan looked on, for an America where "ALL of God's children, *black* men and *white* men, *Jews* and *Gentiles*, *Protestants* and *Cath-o-lics*, will be able to join hands, and sing in the words of the old Negro spiritual, free at *last*, *free at last*, THANK GOD A-MIGHTY, *we are free at last!*" If Baez told the same story in her music, it was in a different language.

"Fair young maid, all in a garden," began the probably seventeenth-century ballad "John Riley" as it appeared in 1960 on *Joan Baez*, her first album. It's the quieting of the tale as Baez moves it on, a little melodic pattern on her guitar flitting by like a small bird as a hushed bass progression follows it like a cat, even more than her voice—the voice of someone already gone, but walking the earth to warn the living—that told the listener then, and can tell a listener now, that he or she has stumbled into a different country. For years, across the South, civil rights workers had been jailed, beaten, killed, their homes fire-bombed, the churches where they gathered burned to the ground. Nine years before, in 1954, the Supreme Court had ruled unanimously that the segregation of public schools was unconstitutional, that it was an affront to the nation as it had constituted itself, that it would have to end; with Federal judges slowly ordering that the decision be taken off the page and enforced where people actually lived, district by district, year by year, black children attempting to enter previously all-white schools were now pushed, spat upon, and cursed by vicious mobs that would have killed them if the National Guard had not been at their side. From a letter written in July 1964 by an intern in the office of Representative Phillip Burton, of San Francisco, who, with black Americans throughout Mississippi denied the right to vote under what was still called White Democracy, had taken it upon himself to stand in Washington for those in Mississippi who had no representative willing to speak for them:

Burton went down to Miss to look things over, and issued a lot of statements. He was sure that the Mississippi delegation was going to blast him on the floor of the House when Congress reconvened (Monday). Therefore, I got the assignment of researching a comprehensive indictment of Miss while he went on a rest vacation. I waded through six volumes of the 1961 US Civil Rights report, the five hundred–page 1963 report, three special rights reports on Mississippi, and a few other things. I also read through the NY Times from June 1 to July 16, which is a four-foot high stack. I did that to find all the anti-Negro violence in Miss in that time. In that month and a half I discovered seven murders of Negroes by whites, about 20 church burnings and bombings, innumerable beatings and arrests. Also, there have been fourteen Negroes killed in Miss since January that no one has ever been brought to trial for—all were connected with CR. I also discovered that there were thirteen counties in Mississippi that do not have even one Negro registered to vote, although Negroes make up as much as 70 percent of the population.

The nation was coming to a verge, where it would have to make good on its promises of liberty and equality, or admit, even to itself, that those promises were lies—and in Baez's music, this social fact was at once affirmed and suspended. At the time, for the high school and college students who were buying Baez's albums as charms and trances, it was like waking up as an adult, or nearly so, to discover that all the fairy tales of your childhood were true—and that, if you wished, instead of the career or the war awaiting you, you could live them out. In a few old songs, making a drama of hiding and escape, material defeat and spiritual conquest, investing that drama with the passion of her voice and the physical presence of the body that held it, she seemed to guide you toward a crack in the invisible wall around your city. What would it mean, people all across the country asked the music they were hearing, as the music asked them, as they pressed that music upon friends as both a talisman and a test of affinities, to feel anything so deeply?

By 1963 Baez's face was familiar everywhere; she'd been on the cover of *Time*. In New Jersey she was appearing under an open-air tent, in the sort of theatre-in-the-round that had become a flag of right-thinking sitting down. She sang, and after a bit she said, "I want to introduce a friend of mine," and out came a scruffy-looking guy with a guitar. He looked dusty and indistinct; his shoulders were hunched and he acted slightly embarrassed.

He sang a few songs in a rough but modest, self-effacing voice, and then he sang one or two with Joan Baez. Then he left and she finished her show—though in those days, the high days of the folk movement, no one would have referred to anything a folk singer did by so vulgar a term as show. It was a concert, an invitation, a gathering, a celebration of val-

ues—values of tradition and fraternity, equality and con-
cord—a coming together of like-minded spirits, a ritual, and
that was the meaning of that round stage, meant to recall
plays and sings in medieval villages, after the harvest was
brought in. No one in front, no one in back, no privilege, no
shame.

I barely noticed the end of the show. I was transfixed. I
was confused—a reaction that people who've paid attention
to Bob Dylan's work across the course of his career know all
too well.

This person had stepped onto someone else's stage, and
while in some ways he seemed as ordinary as any of the people under the tent or the dirt around it, something in his
demeanor dared you to pin him down, to sum him up and
write him off, and you couldn't do it. From the way he sang
and the way he moved, you couldn't tell where he was from,
where he'd been, or where he was going—though the way he
moved and sang made you want to know all of those things.
"Oh, my name it is nothing/ My age it means less," he sang
that day, beginning his song "With God on Our Side." "The
place that I come from/ Is called the Midwest."

As with other songs he would sing in the years to come,
this was one of those strange compositions, one of those
uncanny performances, in which the whole of what is happening comes through instantly and irrevocably. You hear
the song once, on a car radio, with the singer's voice only
inches from your face, or at a concert, the singer many rows

away but physically present—and you understand it completely. As with a face glimpsed on the street or an image in a movie from the edge of the frame, enough of the song roots itself in your memory that you can play it back to yourself at any time. Good Nashville songs do this—Garth Brooks's 1992 "That Summer," Alan Jackson's 2001 "Where Were You (When the World Stopped Turning)"—because they're built like commercials, with cues that tell a listener what inevitably follows from whatever she has just heard even before she has registered that she has heard it. What the person singing that afternoon was doing was somewhat different, or rather he was doing the same thing on a stage so much greater that the nature of the act was altogether changed. He was telling those who were listening a story they already knew, but in a manner that made the story new—that made the familiar unstable, and the comforts of familiarity unsure.

In a simple song, the singer was retelling the story of all American history, as he and his audience had learned it in the public schools of the postwar 1940s and '50s: the common schools, as they used to be called, where with history textbooks reassuringly worn by your older brothers and sisters, even your parents, the children of the rich and the children of the poor were together initiated into the great narrative, that, war by war, had made the country a nation. Clumsily, but with a deference toward the story he was retelling that took the clumsiness away, starting with the Civil War the singer left nothing out: the Indian wars, the First World War, the Second World War, even the Spanish-American War. His audience had already learned the lesson, and it had also forgotten it; now the tale was brought back to consciousness, but it was deformed. As the young man on the stage named our wars, he did so to describe their significance, and their significance was that regardless of the cause or the purpose of the specific conflict in which the United States had engaged itself, the nation was proved right. With God on its side it could not be otherwise. The modesty of the recital lulled the listener back into childhood, which was not as simple as you might have been told it was. Even in the fourth or fifth grade, reading your history textbook—by means of that act becoming a citizen, and thus you as much as anyone embodying the nation itself—you might have done so with a certain suspicion that no one could be quite so blessed, or lucky, but by not disputing the claim you would accept it anyway. Who was there to argue with? Yourself?

Because the singer seemed to slightly infuse every familiar image with doubt, the song came across like ice breaking. It was someone on the edge of a crowd listening to a man running for office; someone who, as the speaker told the people what he thought they wanted to hear, said quietly, but in such a way that what was said ran through the crowd like a rumor, with everyone quieting so that they could hear the next word, that not a word the candidate was saying was true. The result wasn't that the people in the crowd agreed; it was that they began to think it over.

As a performer, with "God on Our Side" the singer had at once addressed the audience and taken his place in it. He created a drama in which you no longer knew quite where you were even as you understood everything that was being said. All at once he confirmed your identity and took it away.

It was an anonymous drama. The singer disappeared into the old books he shared with the people listening, and the drama paid off on the song's promise: as the person on the stage sang, as if he had not only read about the wars he spoke of but witnessed them, you couldn't tell his age. You could imagine him a hundred years old, or older than that. Seeing him plain, he might have been seventeen, he might have been twenty-eight—and to an eighteen-year-old like me, that was someone very old.

As on *Time Out of Mind*, made of newly composed songs that when one brings certain moods to them can sound older than Bob Dylan or the person listening will ever be, Dylan had announced himself under the same shape-shifting shadow. On *Bob Dylan*, his first album, released in March 1962, he appeared as a tramp: not the Chaplin tramp he often drew from onstage in those days, but someone who had slept in hobo jungles, seen men drink themselves mad with Sterno, and forgotten the names of people who for a night had seemed like the best friends anyone could ever have. Many of the songs are funny ("I been around this whole country," he says at the start of "Pretty Peggy-O" of the place-name that in 1962 was a folk signpost, "but I never yet found Fennario"); all in all the album was a collection of old songs about death. They dare the singer—*What makes you think you can sing me?* Blind Lemon Jefferson rises out of the grave in Wortham, Texas, where he's slept since 1929, to ask this middle-class Jewish kid, born Robert Zimmerman in 1941, what he thinks he's doing with his "See That My Grave Is Kept Clean" on his lips—and the singer throws the dare back: *How can you deny me what is mine?* In the early sixties, the Cambridge folk singer Geoff Muldaur was so caught up by Jefferson's plea that he told all his friends he was going to travel to Jefferson's grave with a broom and sweep it off. Dylan's performance of the song gave the lie to the conceit. *Why should I sweep his grave? I'm in it.*

That first album appeared seven months before the Cuban Missile Crisis, when—as then–Secretary of Defense Robert McNamara would tell the nation four decades later, in the film *The Fog of War*, in a voice in which you could hear his knowledge still struggling against his disbelief—the world truly did come within inches and minutes of an actual nuclear war. But it was a time when almost everyone assumed that nuclear war would take place somewhere, sometime, if not everywhere for all time. It was a time when black Americans, and white Americans who joined with them, risked their lives, and sometimes had them taken, whenever they raised their voices. It was a time when such people risked their lives when they walked forward when they were ordered to turn back, when they took a step outside the country into which they had been born and into a new country—and that new country was nothing more than the country they and everyone else had been promised nearly two centuries before: a promise that, like a twenty-year-old from the mining town of Hibbing, Minnesota, taking possession of the songs of dead blues singers, they now understood they would have to keep for themselves. Death is real, the person singing on *Bob Dylan* said; knocking on a door perhaps built especially for that purpose, the sound Dylan made—in moments hysterical, callow, too cool—could have seemed ridiculous, but it didn't. The singer wasn't ridiculous because he was right.

That day in New Jersey in 1963, Dylan's voice was scraped and twisting, and not quite present, as if it were more a suggestion he was making than a claim he was staking. It was a voice that called up blocked roads and half-lit labyrinths, full of hints and beckonings, all cut with a sly, distant humor, a sense of secrets too good to tell out loud. The performance was unassuming, faceless, unique, perverse, pleasurable, and scary all at the same time.

When the show was over I spotted the singer, whose name I hadn't caught, crouching behind the tent—there was no backstage, no guards, no protocols; this was, for an afternoon, that medieval village, with people gathered around Joan Baez, trying to remind her of a night they'd pulled her car out of the snow or brought her mother candy—so I went up to him. He was trying to light a cigarette. It was windy, and his hands were shaking; he wasn't paying attention to anything but the match. I was just dumbfounded enough to open my mouth. "You were terrific," I said brightly. "I was shit," he said, not looking up. "I was just shit." I didn't know what to say to that, so I walked off, casting an eye at Baez's gleaming black Jaguar XKE, in those days the sexiest car on the road.

The reason I tell this ordinary story is that this first time I heard Bob Dylan's voice was only the first first time.

"Ladies and gentlemen, please welcome the poet laureate of rock 'n' roll. The voice of the promise of the sixties counterculture. The guy who forced folk into bed with rock, who donned makeup in the seventies and disappeared into a haze of substance abuse, who emerged to find *Jay-sus*, who was written off as a has-been in the late eighties—and who suddenly shifted gears, releasing some of the strongest music of his career beginning in the late nineties. Ladies and gentlemen, please welcome Columbia Recording Artist, Bob Dylan!"

That summation—boilerplate as it first appeared in the Buffalo *News* in 2001, noting an upcoming Bob Dylan concert in nearby Hamburg, New York, but hilarious, telling, cutting and true as, appropriated as Dylan's official introduction, it came out of the wings in Madison Square Garden in 2002—is as good as any. As pure media shock, instantly producing the displacement that occurs when the conventions of one form replace the conventions of another, it cleared the territory.

Though throughout the years Bob Dylan has, as his stage announcement suggests, performed as an employee in his own touring factory who forgot to punch his own time clock; as a man on a treadmill, each step forward leaving him not even one step behind, which would at least be movement: as someone trading on his name and his legend and offering nothing more. He has also performed as if his name means nothing and his age means less. Again and again he has come onto a stage and thrown off all baggage of fame or respect, familiarity and expectation, all the burdens and prizes that come when a performer acts as if he knows exactly how little he can get away with, or aims to please and does. Again and again, he has refused to give an audience what it paid for.

Those moments of rejection, of Bob Dylan clearing his decks or clearing his throat, occur all across his career. On high school stages in Hibbing with his rock 'n' roll band the Golden Chords, playing piano and singing the Hollywood Flames' "Buzz-Buzz-Buzz"—and in coffeehouses in Minneapolis and Greenwich Village in the early 1960s, when in his hands such folk-scene standards as "No More Auction Block" or "Handsome Molly" became not references to a flight from slavery or the allure of a faithless lover but the thing itself, the past invading the Gaslight Cafe like a curse. At the Newport Folk Festival on 25 July 1965, when "Like a Rolling Stone," which had entered the charts the day before, was first performed, to boos, hysterics, cheers, shouts of abuse, and silence, and in the Free Trade Hall in Manchester,

England, in May 1966, when Dylan and his band, an errant rockabilly blues quintet from Toronto called the Hawks, conducted a war with a crowd outraged over their mocking betrayal of the eternal troubadour—a war that culminated when a fan stood up before the six on the stage and shouted "Judas!" a shout the six followed with more than seven minutes of "Like a Rolling Stone," played as if it were a ship fighting its way out of a storm. Up in the Catskills in the summer of 1967 with a regrouped Hawks, about to become the Band, practicing alchemy on the old American folk language of nonsensical warnings and absurdist tall tales—and throughout a two-week evangelical crusade at the Warfield Theatre in San Francisco in 1979. With a rehearsal for "Blind Willie McTell" in 1983, a visionary song about a dead blues singer, the doom his country is calling down upon itself, and the route of the singer's escape—and with the traditional songs Dylan began performing on stage in the late 1980s, as if seeking comrades in the likes of "When First Unto This Country" and "Eileen Aroon" as crowds barked and hollered, ignoring every word he sang. From the versions of commonplace blues and folk tunes he recorded on bare, unproduced albums in 1992 and 1993, each number turned into a kind of detective story, now with the singer the private eye and the song the case to be broken, then the other way around—to the burnt ground and retreating images of homecoming in *Time Out of Mind*. "I got new eyes," he sang there in "Highlands." "Everything looks far away." It was 1997: he was

singing a sixteen-minute song as if he were rewriting a single
floating blues fragment, best sung in 1940 by Lucious Curtis
in Natchez, Mississippi, in a jaunty style:

> Babe I went
> And I stood up
> On some high old lonesome hill
> Babe I went and I stood up on some
> High old lonesome hill
> And looked down on the house
> Where I used to live

Coursing through these incidents and many more like
them—incidents in which folk music was found and supposedly cast off like worn-out clothes; when a huge pop audience was confronted, challenged, and escaped; when the
oldest strains of American language and ritual were reclaimed
and reinvented; moments when religion replaced both
romance and everyday life, and then when a certain stoic,
Puritan piety became less an altar call than a way of judging
the worth of any new day—was an enormous, motley,
inescapable cast of characters, a whole world: Ma Rainey and
Bill Clinton, John F. Kennedy and Brigitte Bardot, Charley
Patton and Bobby Vee, St. Augustine and the Fifth Daughter
on the Twelfth Night, Hattie Carroll and William
Zantzinger, Tom Paine and John Wesley Harding, Robert
Burns and Stagger Lee, Poor Howard and Georgia Sam, Lyn-

don B. Johnson and the frog that one day up and married a mouse, the murdered civil rights leader Medgar Evers, in a song directly named for him, but also, hiding in a song that featured T. S. Eliot, Albert Einstein, and the Phantom of the Opera, the three black circus workers lynched in 1920 in Duluth, Minnesota, where Bob Dylan was born.* And not only their like. In that cast of characters, running alongside the train of Bob Dylan's music as it runs through the decades—people jumping on, people jumping off, perhaps meeting it again the next time the train made a stop at what-

---

* In September 1918 in Duluth, near the end of the First World War, a group calling itself the Knights of Liberty claimed responsibility for kidnapping and then tarring and feathering an anti-war Finnish immigrant, Olli Kinkkonen, to set an example for those who might avoid the draft; the report was not confirmed until two weeks later, when Kinkkonen's body was found hanging from a tree outside of town, covered with tar and feathers. His death was ruled a suicide. Then on 15 June 1920, six black workers with John Robinson's Circus, passing through Duluth for a one-night performance, were arrested and accused of raping a nineteen-year-old white woman who had attended the show the night before. Between five and ten thousand citizens stormed the Duluth jail and seized on Elias Clayton, Elmer Jackson, and Isaac McGhie as the guilty men, and despite the pleas of the Rev. William Powers of Sacred Heart Cathedral hung them from a single light post. Afterwards members of the crowd posed with the bodies for photographs; one was made into one of the most widely circulated of the many lynching postcards that were popular at the time as "Wish You Were Here" greetings and signs of home-town pride. In 2002, the city of Duluth erected a memorial to the murdered men, three seven-foot-high bronze sculptures designed by Carla Stetson; it was denounced on the Web site V Dare as an attempt "to make whites ashamed of their race." Dylan's paternal grandparents had settled in Duluth in 1907; on 15 June 1920 his father, Abraham Zimmerman, was eight. It is not known if he or his parents attended the lynching.

ever place one called home—are more than forty years of listeners, fans, musicians, the devoted and the curious, the
enthralled and the bored, the outraged and the confirmed,
with, as surely as night follows day, the confirmed finding
themselves outraged around the next turn.

In that sense, in a country that is settled, a country that
like an old and painted whore can still pretend to innocence,
Bob Dylan has moved from state to state and decade to
decade as if nothing was settled, as if everything remains up
for grabs. By doing so he raised the stakes of life all around
himself. As often as not he has done this with the affirmation
of an absolute lurking somewhere up ahead or far behind.
Depending on the song in which that affirmation appears or
on the way in which on a given night a song is performed, it
is an affirmation of all or nothing: an absolute that can make
it plain that the story Dylan takes the stage to tell is an
unwritten book, a story that remains to be made up out of
whole cloth by whoever has the nerve to do so, or that the
story is a closed book, locked and sealed, that the story was
finished and fixed long before it occurred to him to tell it,
and that as he stands on the stage nothing remains to him but
to take the stage down.

It's when a performer dramatizes such extremes that any
time can be the first time—and of all the first times Bob
Dylan has enacted, there is one in which he seemed both to
take the stage down and read from an unwritten book, all at
once. It was at the Grammy Awards show, on 20 February

1991. As television, it was a break from the round-the-clock coverage of the seemingly magical bombing of Baghdad, an evening falling square in the middle of the first Iraqi-American war, an evening of music and self-congratulation that for all of its speeches and applause was drowned out by the sound of an entire nation cheering for certain victory, cheering for itself. On this night, Bob Dylan was to receive a Lifetime Achievement Award, and so before the ceremonies he came onstage with a four-man band to play one song.

They came onto the stage as if they were sneaking onto it; as if, somehow, they might get on and off without being noticed. The band members were dressed in dark suits, with fedoras pulled down; they looked like supremely confident small-time Chicago hipster gangsters who'd spent the last ten years in the same bar waiting for the right deal to break and finally said the hell with it. Who were these people? Bob Dylan was there to pick up his award, yes, but now the whole frame of reference was gone. What exactly he was doing there, on that stage, in this stopped moment, was a complete mystery.

The mystery was there to be deepened; with the first beat the band turned off the lights. They roared into a song, with Dylan slurring the words, breaking them down and smashing them up until they functioned as pure force. Stray lines of excitement, pleasure, and dread streamed out of the sound like loose wires. As the song went on it picked up speed, momentum; the sound was crude in the beginning and raw at the end. Dylan chanted like a madman on the street, as if he

were speaking in tongues: was this a sermon, a curse, a juke-
joint stomp, a firefight? The Rev. J. M. Gates of Atlanta
preaching "The End of the World and Time Will Be No
More" on a Victor 78 in 1927? John Brown writing "the
crimes of this *guilty, land: will* never be purged *away;* but with
Blood" in 1859, on the day of his execution? A highlight of
the forthcoming Columbia album *Having a Rave Up with Bob
Dylan?* It's fun to imagine that half of the millions who were
watching were wondering what the song was, and that the
rest were so lost in the music they didn't care—more likely,
anyone who did care was split in half. The song was hidden
in its own music; the surge of the music overrode the setting
and joined itself to the events taking place offstage. And
then, perhaps two minutes into the three and a half the performance would take, the song began to reveal itself. It was
"Masters of War," Dylan's most unforgiving, damning anti-
war song, from *The Freewheelin' Bob Dylan*, his second album,
from 1963, but in 1963 it was slow, stolid, the very template
of the protest song, almost a speech, a funeral oration: "I'll
stand over your grave 'til I'm sure that you're dead."*

---

* In May 2004 *Mojo* magazine ranked "Masters of War" number one on a chart
of "The 100 Greatest Protest Songs." Directly behind were Pete Seeger's "We
Shall Overcome" (1963), James Brown's "Say it Loud—I'm Black and I'm
Proud" (1968), the Sex Pistols' "God Save the Queen" (1977), and Billie Holi-
day's "Strange Fruit" (1939). Also included were Eddie Cochran's "Summertime
Blues" (1958), Lesley Gore's "You Don't Own Me" (1964), and Negativland's
"Christianity Is Stupid" (1987); inexplicably omitted were the Boomtown Rats'
"I Don't Like Mondays" (1980), Carl Perkins's "Blue Suede Shoes" (1956), Barry
McGuire's "Eve of Destruction," and at least a dozen other Bob Dylan songs.

But now the song didn't merely say that—or rather in the cacophony of the music it barely said it at all. The song made it happen. It put you next to the grave site, dared you to stand on it, all but handed you a shovel so that you might dig up the grave and lay out the corpse for dogs. And it didn't matter if you didn't catch a word, if you didn't know the song, if you didn't have a personal Western Union in your head to deliver its message. In the hall where the Grammys were being handed out that night, the performance said that real life was elsewhere, that it was dangerous, that life was a runaway train and you were on that train whether you'd bought a ticket or not. You were fated to reach its final destination, regardless of where, when you rose that morning, you might have flattered yourself to imagine you were going. That night, a song Bob Dylan had recorded almost thirty years before was performed for the first time, and in the same way, that night, it was performed for the last time.

It was this sort of drama that "Like a Rolling Stone" set loose in Bob Dylan's music—the reach for that moment when the stakes of life are raised. People recognized that from the first. "The first time I heard it was when we went to L.A. It was number one in L.A. I'd never heard of the song and I'd never heard of Bob Dylan. We were driving down Hollywood Boulevard or somewhere and the song comes out. We were with a whole bunch of people and everybody started screaming and I said, 'What's this all about' and they said turn up the radio." So said Steve Cropper, guitarist for Booker T.

and the MG's, in 1965 the leading soul band in the country, but for what he said he could have been anybody. The drama was instantaneous, overwhelming, a story that sucked you in and, for an escape, offered only a ride on a final blast from a harmonica that was like a riderless surfboard shooting off the top of a wave. There was a kind of common epiphany, a gathering of a collective unconscious: the song melted the mask of what was beginning to be called youth culture, and even more completely the mask of modern culture as such. "Anybody can be specific and obvious," Dylan said of the song in early 1966, speaking to the jazz critic Nat Hentoff.

That's always been the easy way. The leaders of the world take the easy way. It's not that it's so difficult to be unspecific and less obvious; it's just that there's nothing, absolutely nothing, to be specific and obvious *about*. My older songs, to say the least, were about nothing. The newer ones are about the same nothing—only as seen inside a bigger thing, perhaps called nowhere.

In "Like a Rolling Stone," that nowhere was a rising tide. Writing in 1985, the British critic Wilfred Mellers caught the feeling: the music, he said, leaves "one agog for what comes next." Not everyone; describing the song in 1967, at a lecture at the University of California at Berkeley, the great Los Angeles record producer Phil Spector argued that while "It's always very satisfying to rewrite the chords to 'La Bamba,'" what "Like a Rolling Stone" needed was a bigger sound—by

which Spector meant his own Wall of Sound. He drew a distinction between recordings that could be defined as "a
record" and those that could be defined as "an idea," noting in
a modest aside that a recording that was both a record and an
idea—his production of the Crystals' "Da Doo Ron Ron," he
suggested—"can rule the world." "Like a Rolling Stone," he
said, was only an idea.*

If "Like a Rolling Stone" was not a wall of sound, it was a
river of sound in its verses, and a mountain of sound in its
refrain: river deep, mountain high. Across nearly forty years
of trying, I've never understood Phil Spector's theory (maybe
somewhere there's a tape of the lecture he gave that night;
maybe he *explained*), but I've always figured he knew something I didn't. Assume he was right; if "Like a Rolling Stone"
was not a record, it was an event: not the event of its commercial release, or even the event made when it reached the
public at large, but event of the drama generated by the performance itself. And it was as such an event that it joined
with the other events that made its time.

------

* "His favorite song is "Like a Rolling Stone," Spector told Jann Wenner of
Rolling Stone in 1969, elaborating on what he'd said two years before, "and it
stands to reason because that's his grooviest song, as far as songs go. It may not
be his grooviest message. It may not be the greatest thing he ever wrote, but I
can see why he gets the most satisfaction out of it, because rewriting 'La
Bamba' chord changes is always a lot of fun and anytime you can make a Number One record and rewrite those changes, it is very satisfying." With George
Harrison on guitar and Charlie Daniels on bass, Dylan recorded a frat-house-
basement version of "Da Doo Ron Ron" in 1970: "I met her on a Monday . . .
I saw her last Friday . . . "

CHAPTER TWO

Top 40 Nation

When you made the charts in 1965, you became part of a small but dynamic world. It changed every week, just like the world of work and family life, politics and war. As in the world of work, family, politics, and war, certain of the elements of the pop world—disc jockey patter and commercials, the rituals of contests and pranks—barely changed at all, and other elements changed so radically they hijacked memory, to the point that whatever happened the week before could seem to have happened years ago. This was Top 40 radio: city by city, from one end of the country to the other, a true forum, in 1965 more open to anyone, known or unknown, black or white, northerner or southerner, American or foreigner, male or female, than any other cultural medium—never mind business, religion, or college.

The outside world, the apparent real world, changed very quickly. There were 27,000 U.S. troops, including the first combat troops on the ground, in Vietnam in March 1965, just three months after Secretary of Defense Robert McNamara told President Johnson that the war was "going to hell"; by the end of the year there would be 170,000. Voting rights marches in Selma, Alabama, in the first part of the year, met with horrifying police violence, still allowed most Americans to see the Negro problem as a southern problem, not an American problem; with the riots in Watts in Los Angeles in August, the black riot, the police riot, which left thirty-four people dead and a sector of the city destroyed, the nation woke up to the news that the country no longer had a map. Riots in black ghettos in the big eastern cities—that, white Americans thought they understood. But what did Negroes in Los Angeles have to complain about, aside from a police force that from the beginning of the century was as racist and as murderous as any in the country? "Even the poorest streets had houses with lawns and running water to keep the grass green," Walter Mosley had his Watts detective Easy Rawlins remember in *Little Scarlet*, looking back in 2004 to the world as it was thirty-nine years before. "There were palm trees on almost every block and the residential sidewalks were lined with private cars. Every house had electricity to see by and natural gas to cook with. There were televisions, radios, washing machines, and dryers in houses up and down the street"—but as the critic Guy Debord wrote of Watts from

Paris, "comfort will never be comfortable enough for those who seek what is not on the market." Yes, it had all started with a crowd gathering around a routine traffic stop on a hot night, and then, as Easy Rawlins explained it to himself, "one symptom of a disease that had silently infected the city; a virus that made people suddenly unafraid of the consequences of standing up for themselves." "It was not so much that Negroes had *finally* had enough," the critic Stanley Crouch, at nineteen on the streets in Watts in 1965, wrote in 2004; "they had *always* had enough." "Almost every black man, woman, and child you meet feels that anger," Rawlins says to a white woman. "But they've never let on, so you've never known. This riot was sayin' it out loud for the first time. That's all. Now it's said and nothing will ever be the same. That's good for us, no matter what we lost. And it could be good for white people too. But they have to understand just what happened here."

Sometimes the country of the charts changed faster than that. At its most intense it was not a reflection of the events chronicled in the newspapers—or even those events left out of the papers but talked about anyway—but a version of them: the moronic, the clichéd, and the vapid suddenly blindsided by the beautiful, which for a moment was the truth.

The first new number one hit of the year was Petula Clark's "Downtown," a charming song about freedom that fit right into commercials advertising the thrill of dressing somewhat differently, wearing your hair slightly longer, or taking a day off. You can't change your life, the song said, but for a day or a night you can escape it. Everybody liked the song, and nobody cared about it—at least until the song went back on the air on the East Coast in September 2001, the week after the terrorist attacks in downtown New York: an act of defiance, an awful joke, or a computer programmed the year before, nobody knew. With Petula Clark in his ear, Bob Dylan was in the studio with a band, recording "Subterranean Homesick Blues," "On the Road Again," "Outlaw Blues," and "Bob Dylan's 115th Dream," noisy rock 'n' roll songs that along with others that were not noisy would in March appear on the album *Bringing It All Back Home*.

On January 30, a week after "Downtown" hit the top—and three weeks before gunmen from the Nation of Islam assassinated the apostate Malcolm X, once the scary, unsatisfiable public face of the Black Muslims, then the traitor who had discovered that founder Elijah Muhammad, like so many American cult leaders before him, had gathered his flock less as a community of believers than as a harem—Sam Cooke's "A Change Is Gonna Come" went into the charts. Like "Downtown," it was a song about freedom. It was also about racism, and like a call from the grave to the marchers in Selma, who were, some of them, digging their own: a star in white America but a hero in black America, Cooke had been shot to death by a motel manager in Watts the month before.

Inspired by Bob Dylan's 1963 "Blowin' in the Wind," which was itself inspired by the Civil Rights Movement ("Geez," Cooke said, "a white boy writing a song like that?")*, but an infinitely better song, "A Change Is Gonna Come" was recorded on New Year's Day, 1964, in Los Angeles, with the great New Orleans drummer Earl Palmer, at the end of the sessions for Cooke's *Ain't That Good News*. Early the next month Cooke performed it on the *Tonight Show*. The orchestration was pure Hollywood, a movie theme, maybe *Cabin in the Sky* or *Porgy and Bess*, maybe the movie Randy Newman always said his song "Sail Away" was meant to be: stirring, with strings enacting an inevitable triumph, horns enacting conflict, a kettle drum enacting doom, or a martyr's curse on his native land. Singing in a voice as clear as water, rich and expansive—"It was the *tone* of his voice," Rod Stewart once said. "Not the phrasing or whatever: just the tone"—bending syllables like staircases in a dream, disappearing under your feet as you try to climb them, stretching out the word "long" until it became what before it only signified, Cooke looked the country in the face.

---

* "A folk trio out of Greenwich Village was riding the charts with a song called 'Blowin' in the Wind' that caught and held Sam's attention," Daniel Wolff wrote in 1995 in *You Send Me: The Life & Times of Sam Cooke*, speaking of 1963. "Peter, Paul & Mary were a long way from rock & roll (which they disliked and mocked) but it wasn't the group or the folk poetry of Bob Dylan's lyrics that struck Cooke. It was the fact that a tune could address civil rights *and* go to #2 on the pop charts."

Then I go to my brother
And I say brother, he'p me please
But he winds up
Knockin' me
Back down on my knees

Ohhhhhhhhhh—
There been times, that I thought
I couldn't last for long
But now I think I'm able, to
Carry on
It's been a long
A long time comin', but I know
A change gone come
Oh yes it will

Never rising higher than number 31, the B side of the
number 7 "Shake," it was the greatest soul record ever made,
and everybody who heard it knew it. It wasn't a sentimental
judgment, because Cooke was dead; it wasn't a judgment at
all. It was a recognition. The music didn't make you sorry
Cooke was dead; it made you glad that he had lived, made
you feel privileged to have shared the earth with him. This
record wasn't the real world invading the phony little con-
struct of the pop world to remind it of the travails outside; it
was the pop world seizing something from the real world and
sending it back, transformed, the absolute of art negating the

hesitations and demurrers of ordinary speech, or, for as long as the record played, the limits of the real world itself.*

---

* On 28 March 2004, at *Apollo at 70: A Hot Night in Harlem*, an all-star benefit for the Apollo Theater Foundation, Natalie Cole sang a song into the ground, there was a tribute to Ray Charles, and then the actor and civil rights activist Ossie Davis, in his eighties and speaking as if he had all the time in the world, took the stage. "At the end of the fifties," he said, "the Civil Rights Movement was growing very insistent—hot and heavy. My generation was involved, challenging America's deep racial divide. We marched, we prayed, we preached—and fought—for freedom. Music became a significant force in bringing these issues to light, and bringing the people together." So, far, Davis was simply mouthing awards-show blather; then he took a turn. "A young singer by the name of Sam Cooke was dominating the charts," he said as footage of Cooke performing with more than a dozen singers and dancers appeared on the theater screen. "One day, Sam heard a song that asked, a mighty important question." As the sound came up on the screen, you could hear that Cooke was singing "Blowin' in the Wind": "Yes, and how many deaths will it take till he knows/ That too many people have died?/ The answer, my friend, is blowing in the wind"—and to hear Cooke's seamless voice inside Dylan's "blowin'" was to hear the song as something new. "It prompted him," Davis said, "to write what is perhaps his most heartfelt and moving work: 'A Change . . . Is Gonna Come.' A song which became an anthem for the Civil Rights Movement. To perform it for us tonight is someone I've had the pleasure of introducing *before*"—and Davis filled up the word with weight, finally hitting his rhetorical stride—"when we were together once, on that historic day in Washington, D.C., in nineteen, sixty, three, when Dr. Martin Luther King told us about the dream he wanted to share with all America. I'm pleased—nay, happy—to reintroduce this artist again tonight. Ladies and gentlemen, Bob Dylan."

With his band in darkness—hatted guitarist and stand-up bassist, hatless guitarist and drummer—Dylan stood behind an electric piano and went right into the song. The sound of his voice was the sound of shoe leather scraping a sidewalk; the song was out of Dylan's vocal range, so he brought it into his range as a comrade. At first, with a circular guitar pattern and taps on a woodblock, the song came out soupy. Slowing the pace as radically as he could, Dylan gave himself space to drag out certain words, to flatten the melody, and

"Downtown" was followed at the top of the charts by Phil Spector's magnificent production of the Righteous Brothers' "You've Lost that Lovin' Feeling," and then Gary Lewis and the Playboys' "This Diamond Ring," written by Al Kooper, who four months later would sit down at a Hammond organ to play on "Like a Rolling Stone." Years later, Kooper would claim that he had written "This Diamond Ring" as a serious soul ballad, and even recorded a version to prove it; in 1965 it was the apotheosis of inanity. Gary Lewis's voice was whiny, the sound was tinny, and to the millions who could not stop themselves from singing along it was far more embarrassing than anything Gary's father Jerry had ever done, and he knew something about embarrassment. As thousands of people from Selma, and all over the country, and from beyond the country, marched out of the town and, under the protection of the Federal government, walked the fifty-four miles to the state capitol in Montgomery to demand an end to disenfranchisement, a Constitutional

---

[continued] by the second verse—the singer in front of a movie theater, being told he couldn't come in—you saw someone on a WPA stage from the thirties, bare except perhaps for a backdrop of a setting sun. The performance was made of dignity and authority—qualities that, as Dylan sang, were passed from him to the song to Cooke and back again to him. The gorgeous, sophisticated record Cooke had made four decades before was now rough, primitive; where Cooke was a nightclub prophet, Dylan was a tramp on the street, a prophet content to say his piece and disappear. That's how he sounded; in a rakish, cutaway beige jacket, pink satin shirt, black string tie, and pencil moustache, he looked like a card shark.

crime that four months later would be ended by the Voting Rights Act, passed by Congress and signed by Lyndon B. Johnson as the greatest legacy of his presidency—one of the marchers Joan Baez, one of them a one-legged man on crutches, one of them a thirty-nine-year-old volunteer from Detroit, Viola Luizzo, who would be shot to death that night from a car full of Klansmen—the Supremes replaced the shimmering smile of the Beatles' "Eight Days a Week" with "Stop! In the Name of Love," their fourth number one record in a row, and so passionate, so well crafted, it made the first three seem like soft-drink jingles.

At the end of April, as Bob Dylan left for a tour of the United Kingdom, where he would find that the songs he sang every night had lost whatever it was that had made them worth singing in the first place, the charts went soft. As hundreds of people continued to be arrested in voting rights demonstrations in the South, Johnson sent Marines into the Dominican Republic to break a democratic revolution, and students and professors speaking out in campus forums mounted the first visible actions against the Vietnam War, with Junior Walker and the All Stars' "Shotgun" and Roger Miller's "King of the Road" floating in the ether, the winners were Herman's Hermits' "Mrs. Brown You've Got a Lovely Daughter"; Wayne Fontana and the Mindbenders' unmindbending "Game of Love"; Freddie and the Dreamers' "I'm Telling You Now," which made "Game of Love" feel like "A Change Is Gonna Come," or rather that "A Change Is Gonna Come" had never existed at all. After that came the Beatles' "Ticket to Ride," a lament with an odd beat, a song that actually registered emotional content—with Gary Lewis and the Playboys chasing the Beatles with "Count Me In," Sam the Sham and the Pharaohs mocking Lewis and everybody else on earth with "Wooly Bully," and Elvis Presley trying to get everyone to calm down with "Crying in the Chapel." But by the end of June, with "Like a Rolling Stone" recorded but not released, the pop world turned. As Bob Dylan has never done, the Byrds reached number one with an adaptation of his "Mr. Tambourine Man," a song included on *Bringing It All Back Home* only a few months before. It was a rich, thick, bottomless sound carrying what could have been the Beach Boys singing, high and fey; in the cadence of its opening the record was an announcement, a signal that it might itself be a version of the change that was going to come. Then the Rolling Stones' "(I Can't Get No) Satisfaction," just three spots above Herman's Hermits' affectionate cover of Sam Cooke's "(What A) Wonderful World," in 1960 a perfect record—and as a record, as opposed to the speech of a prophet, as opposed to "A Change Is Gonna Come," Cooke's best. The Rolling Stones ran the table; they held the top spot on the charts for a month, and by August 10, when they surrendered it to Herman's Hermits' "I'm Henry VIII, I Am," a British music-hall ditty, "Like a Rolling Stone" was on the radio, and Watts was one day from setting a fire that would be seen from the other side of the globe.

Whatever else you want to say about this, it was a field of surprises. In a time of public terror and danger, unparalleled courage and unspeakable venality, truth and lie, and business as usual, in what amounted to a kind of running election there was no definable limit on how little people were willing to accept, or how much they could take. Top 40 radio was a mystery; it was up to the artist to solve it.

CHAPTER THREE

The Man in the Phone Booth

You can find all these people that play music onstage—they definitely have some kind of image, or something, that people came there to see and do, whether it be Lawrence Welk, or Steve McQueen, or Howdy Doody, President Johnson, really, they all expect something—and usually they get what they expect, and what they paid for.

I never promised anybody anything. I used to get up on the stage when I first began playing concerts, and not even know what I was going to do. I used to just walk in from the street. Anything could happen.

Now it's different. Now I want to play the songs—because I actually dig them myself. I was doing a lot of stuff before that I didn't really *dig* . . . stuff which had reasons to be written, which anybody worth anything could see through, which I could see through, and—higher-up people couldn't, *can* see through, but just wouldn't let on, 'cause there is a thing to play a game. So a lot of people play games with me, and call me weird names, because I wrote songs like "With God on Your Side," but—what it *really* meant to write something like that and sing it on the stage has never been brought out or expressed. I've never seen that written anywhere.

—Bob Dylan to Allen Stone, WDTM, Detroit, 24 October 1965

Once an identity is fixed in the public mind or the simple memory of the media it can never be escaped. Just as Bill Clinton's wire-service obituary will begin, "The first president since Andrew Johnson to be impeached," Bob Dylan's will head off with "Most renowned as a protest singer from the 1960s." "Blowin' in the Wind" will be his first song mentioned.

"Kinda ersatz," said a friend in late 1963, when we first heard Dylan's own recording of the already famous protest song. Despite the oddity of anything sounding remotely like Bob Dylan's voice on the radio, he meant that the song sounded as if it were written by the times, not by anyone in particular. Maybe that was why the song, with a melody from the slavery lament "No More Auction Block," as rendered by the glossy folk trio Peter, Paul & Mary—two goateed guitarists and a female singer with long, straight blonde hair (or "two rabbis and a hooker," as the critic Ralph J. Gleason put it)—was such a huge hit. The piece was perhaps not as obvious as it seemed. How long would there be war, it asked, how long would there be racism? If the answer was blowing in the wind, did that mean the answer was where anyone could grasp it, or that the answer would always elude whoever reached for it?

It didn't matter then and it doesn't matter now: the song seemed obvious. And Bob Dylan will never escape it. As with ads for one-hit wonders now reduced to playing local bars you've never heard of, where the promoter always sticks the title of the one hit beneath the name of the act, figuring you might remember the song even if you've forgotten who did it—

EVERY MOTHER'S SON
("COME ON DOWN TO MY BOAT")
Gino's
No cover
One Nite Only

—this notice appeared in *City Pages* in Minneapolis in 1997, for a show at the Minnesota State Fair, no less:

Featuring ... IN PERSON
"Sensational"
BOB DYLAN
"Blowing in the Wind"

Never mind that it's "Blowin'," not "Blowing"; earlier in the year, when the news broke that Dylan might be near death from a heart condition ("I really thought I'd be seeing Elvis," he said when he left the hospital), the newspaper cartoon that would follow the event seemed preordained. You could see a small group of people gathered on a bridge, a scattering of ashes in the air, and the solemn caption: "Now, Bob Dylan too is blowing in the wind."

As the decades went on, Dylan found a way to both give people a song they wanted and bring it to a life it never had when it was new—because in a way it was never new, with the questions used clothes and the missing answer a song-writer's sleight-of-hand. On a live recording Columbia released in 2000—a "field recording," with a bootleg sound, as if caught from somewhere in the crowd—"Blowin' in the Wind" was a free-floating sign, pointing backwards. The song itself was now blowing in the wind; it had long since blown away from its author, and you can hear how people have momentarily attached themselves to it, the author with no more claim to the composition than the audience. He sings as if the song is, somehow, unfamiliar, certainly not as if he owns it. The confidence and condescension of a younger man—*Don't you get it?*—has been replaced by the regret of an older one; singing alongside Dylan, guitarists Charlie Sexton and Larry Campbell take the tune to an aching higher register, and suddenly the song is daring the future to shut it up. Over seven minutes the song is a play—but obituaries don't have room for plays, let alone for anything that, over a life-time, plays out its string.

Thus Bob Dylan, fated to be called weird names even after his death: names like "protest singer." In late 1965, at a press conference in Los Angeles, when Dylan and the Hawks were, as Marlon Brando put it, making the loudest noise he'd ever heard short of a moving freight train, no one asked Dylan about his new music. While friends snickered at his side, one reporter after another asked what he was protest-ing, did he mean what he said, how many protest singers were there ("Forty-two," Dylan said), was it just a trend? *"Il est un* Vietnik," Jean-Pierre Léaud said to Chantal Goya in Jean-Luc Godard's 1966 *Masculin féminin*, explaining Bob Dylan: a beatnik against the Vietnam War. The sleeve of a 1974 boot-leg put its title above the kind of carnival booth that features holes for a man and a woman to join their heads to bodies or costumes painted on plywood—those of the couple from Grant Wood's *American Gothic*, say:

EARLY 60's REVISITED

A Photo of You As You Were—Only $1

Under the empty hole for the woman's head is a braless figure in a turtleneck, pedal pushers, and sandals, holding a sign reading "We Shall Overcome"; a middle-aged Bob Dylan, a look of unhappy acceptance on his face, his head in the space over a figure with a guitar, dressed in jeans, boots, and a sheepskin jacket, waits alone, as if he gets the dollar if you'll pose with him, or as if this is the only way he can still get girls. Already in 1972, as if the sixties were not three years but three decades in the past—or as if "Like a Rolling Stone" had never been sung—the National Lampoon's *Radio Dinner* album had opened with a late-night TV commercial:

Hi! I'm Bob Dylan. Remember those fabulous sixties? The marches, the be-ins, the draft-card burnings, and best of all the music. Well, now Apple House has collected the best of those songs on one album called *Golden Protest*, performed by the original artists that made them famous. You'll thrill to "Society's Child" by Janis Ian! "Pleasant Valley Sunday" by the Monkees! "What Have They Done to the Rain" by the Searchers! "In the Ghetto" by Elvis Presley! "Silent Night/Seven O'Clock News" by Simon and Garfunkel—and who can ever forget that all-time classic, yes, it's Barry McGuire's immortal "Eve of Destruction." And of course, my own "Masters of War." All for the incredibly low price of $3.95. And, if you order now . . .

Behind all of this was a happy desire to acknowledge how impossibly stupid extreme fashions look even months after they go out of style, and a desperate, shamed attempt to pretend that the ideals and convictions that had carried people through the previous years—that had found them living with an intensity and, for some, a creativity that a few years later seemed impossibly fecund—were nothing more than extreme fashions. Bob Dylan, it seemed, had said that wrongs should be made right; if they had not been, if the war was still going on and racism had merely changed shape, those who had recognized themselves through the way Dylan said what he said ("The *sound* of Bob Dylan's voice," the critic Robert Ray once wrote, "changed more people's ideas about the world than his political message did") could best save themselves by painting him as a fool. And the *Radio Dinner* commercial, done with a perfectly aged frog in Dylan's throat, its cadences falling just where they should, was really funny.

Sometimes, as with "The Times They Are A-Changin'," with Dylan in his bard-of-the-people work shirt on the cover of the 1963 album of the same name, his protest songs were programmatic and automatically anthemic, even if unsingable by crowds. More often they came with a cocked eye, with ambiguity and doubt—and a sense of detail that put you in the action. When in the 1990s Dylan sang "The Lonesome Death of Hattie Carroll," from 1963, about the six-month sentence received by a privileged white Marylander who beat a black hotel worker to death with his cane, on occasion the song seemed to slow down: you could almost feel the cane as it moved through the air. Protest songs could be shuffling, laconic stand-up comedy routines, as with the priceless "Talking World War III Blues." The bomb has fallen; the singer takes a Cadillac out of an abandoned dealership. "Good car to drive," he says. "After a war."

Dylan tried to escape the label. "I've never written any

song that begins with the words 'I've gathered you here tonight ...'" he said. Asked about his favorite protest singers, he named lounge singer Eydie Gorme and Robert Goulet, according to legend the artist who first inspired Elvis Presley to shoot out a TV set. Asked for his political opinions, Dylan acted shocked: "I'll bet Tony Bennett doesn't have to go through this kind of thing." He feigned outrage: "Does Smokey Robinson have to answer these questions?" He could have meant that it was ridiculous to ask mere pop singers about the state of the world, or that a black man from Detroit might have more to say about the state of the world than a bohemian from New York City. It didn't matter. He could change his name; he could even change the world, as some commentators insisted, but he couldn't change what he was called.

In *Don't Look Back*, D. A. Pennebaker's documentary film of Dylan's tour of the United Kingdom in the spring of 1965, you see a reporter in a phone booth after a show, dictating a story that could have been written before the show began, if not the year before: "*Sentence.* He is not so much singing as sermonizing. *Colon.* His tragedy, perhaps, is that the audience is preoccupied with song. *Paragraph.* So the bearded boys and the lank-haired girls, all eye-shadow and undertaker makeup, applaud the song and miss the sermon. They are there; they are 'with it.' *Sentence:* But how remote they really are from sit-ins and strikes and scabs. *Paragraph:* 'The times they are a-changin',' sings Dylan. They are when a poet fills a hall." It's

easy to laugh at the string of clichés—but what if those
clichés were being generated by Dylan himself? What if they
were true? What if it wasn't that the audience was missing the
sermon, but that Dylan himself was missing the song? On
that tour, every show began with "The Times They Are A-
Changin'," at that moment in 1965 number 16 on the U.K.
charts, and every time it is a millstone: Pennebaker never
shows more than a few seconds, knowing that to put more of
the song on the screen would be to leave dead air in the film.
Dylan sings "The Lonesome Death of Hattie Carroll";
William Zantzinger's cane merely hits its target. Except for
the end of "Talking World War III Blues," with Dylan reciting
what Lincoln supposedly said about how you can't fool all of
the people all of the time—reciting the words very slowly,
deliberately, upside down and inside out, as if the idea is very
hard to get right, which it is—"Some of the people can be
half right part of the time . . . All of the people can be part
right, *some* of the time . . . Half the people can be part right *all*
of the time . . . But all of the people can't be *all* right, *all of the
time*"—Dylan only comes to life off-stage. "I was singing a lot
of songs I didn't want to play," Dylan told Nat Hentoff in
1966, describing the tour. "I was singing words I didn't really
want to sing." The most damning words were the simplest:
whenever he played a song, Dylan said, "I knew what was
going to happen."

    As Stan Ridgway sang in 2004 in "Classic Hollywood
Ending," "The audience has learned to cheer." The fans knew

their roles; they expected the performer to know his. He did, and he acted it out. It was a ritual of self-confirmation, and the opposite of an event, which is the putting into play of something new, something unpredictable, where anything can happen, where the artist no less than a president subjects himself or herself to what history is made of. "I claim not to have controlled events," as Lincoln certainly wrote on 4 April 1864, "but confess plainly that events have controlled me." Faced with an act—a performance—that breaks the nexus of expectation and result, an audience might rush the stage and attack the performer. The performer might leave the stage in the middle of a song and never come back. The audience might attempt to drive the performer off the stage with denunciation and abuse—which, when Dylan returned to the United Kingdom a year later with the Hawks, is precisely what happened.

It's painful to watch, to see a song die in a singer's mouth, to see people in a crowd cheer the death; it's unsettling to hear the opposite take place, as it did the previous fall. It was a Halloween concert at Philharmonic Hall in New York City. The Vietnam War had not yet seeped into American life; the Beatles had. In the world of folk music, Bob Dylan was now a star; this time he brought Joan Baez onto his stage.

Much of what took place that night in 1964 was as ritual-ized as any show Dylan played in the U.K. the following spring. Two years before, in the Gaslight Cafe in Greenwich Village, as he sang an early version of "A Hard Rain's A-

Gonna Fall," a visionary epic about, people said, the Cuban
Missile Crisis, some in the crowd came in solemnly behind
Dylan on the refrain, as if for a moment the ballad had turned
into a Gregorian chant. The effect was so ghostly it was as if
the Cuban Missile Crisis truly had led to the atomic war
many thought Kennedy thought he was ready for, and that
this, not the ramble of "Talking World War III Blues," was the
sound you heard, after the war. In Philharmonic Hall people
began cheering before Dylan finished the first line of "Who
Killed Davey Moore?" about a boxer beaten to death in the
ring—to show they knew what was coming next, to affirm
that the concert would give them what they expected, that it
would prove to them that they belonged. That same night,
though, Dylan played "It's Alright, Ma (I'm Only Bleeding),"
which he had never played in public before.

Over the years the number would become the most ritu-
alized of any Dylan ever wrote. The harsh, leaping, biting
strum on the guitar, the catalogue of the endless hypocrisies
of modern American life, of advertising, commuters, political
parties, censorship, sexual repression, organized religion,
country clubs, "propaganda all is phony"—all of it would
come to seem like a set up for a single line of the song. By
now, anyone who cares knows what will happen when Dylan
gets to the words "Sometimes even the president of the
United States must have to stand naked." People will stomp
and cheer to show which side they're on—or what messy
choices they're superior to.

The ritual is a trick that time played on the song, as soon enough presidents did find themselves stripped naked, with Lyndon Johnson driven from office, Richard Nixon and his vice president both forced to resign, Jimmy Carter and then George Bush humiliated in defeat, Bill Clinton's every sexual foible exposed to the world, but it is also a trick that for forty years Dylan's audience has played on itself. The song, after all, has outlasted almost as many presidents as Fidel Castro, and as the song is played now on any stage, in any city, you can all but hear people waiting for the line to come up, waiting for the chance to play the part that, by now, the song demands. That is why it is so strange to hear the song as it was played on that Halloween night, before it was a clue to anything, when a twenty-three-year-old Bob Dylan sings "Even the president of the United States sometimes has to stand naked," and nothing happens. The line hangs in the air, in a void it itself has called up, as if it's not obvious what it says. It wasn't obvious: in a few days, almost everyone in Philharmonic Hall old enough to vote would go to the polls to cast their ballots for LBJ, running as the peace candidate against Barry Goldwater, who had flirted with the notion of using atomic weapons in Vietnam. Johnson had yet to be demonized; Nixon, who would disgrace the presidency, had not been elected. Ford had not replaced Nixon, or Carter Ford, or Reagan Carter, or Bush Reagan, or Clinton Bush, or Bush Clinton.

Sometimes, as in a performance in Santa Cruz in 2000,

Dylan was able to take the song back from the events that had controlled it. Here the melody slowly creeps up from silence, coming out of a fog like the memory of an old blue-grass song—"Nine Pound Hammer," maybe. The music bounces forward on a high-stepping beat, until very quickly the syncopation is a finger reaching out of the past, beckoning, and then a hand reaching out of an alley, grabbing your arm. There are light drums, and finger-picking on two acoustic guitars—it's a little folkie chamber orchestra, people around a campfire, a setting rightfully too intimate for anyone to intrude upon with a cheer for anything, though of course when "Sometimes even the president..." comes around some do cheer. "Others say don't hate nothin' at all 'cept ... *hay-tred,*" Dylan sings, the line sticking out of his mouth like a cigar, so sly, so questioning of himself and the people present, so "Did anybody here ever buy that slogan, did anybody put it on a bumper sticker and slap it on their car?" Every verse is thrown away at the end, not with resignation, or bitterness, but with experience, which is still taking place. "What else can you show me?" is sung as if the singer expects neither that there will be something or nothing. For a few minutes at the end the guitars play the song out of itself, as if it is, for this night anyway, no longer a carapace containing a single line, but a chance to find words and rhythms in the song no one has ever heard before.

Soon after that night in the fall of 1964, the song would be stopped cold by its own audience. There was no applause dubbed onto the studio recording that appeared on *Bringing It All Back Home* in March 1965, but "Sometimes even the president..." already implied it. One side of the album led off with "Subterranean Homesick Blues," a two-minute-seventeen-second Chuck Berry–styled comic rant against, among other things, the entire American social system, its "Too Much Monkey Business" leaps disguising, as the music historian David Hajdu seems to have been the first to notice, a lyric rooted in an old Woody Guthrie–Pete Seeger number called "Take It Easy." It was Bob Dylan's first single to reach the pop charts—for one week, at number 39. It was followed on the album by "She Belongs to Me," "Maggie's Farm," "Love Minus Zero/No Limit," "Outlaw Blues," "On the Road Again," and "Bob Dylan's 115th Dream," most of them scratchy, clanging, written with flair, sung with glee, Dylan and his backing musicians in moments thrilled at their own new clatter.

Supposedly made at the suggestion of Dylan's producer Tom Wilson, who as an experiment clumsily dubbed timid, effete electric instrumentation over Dylan's utterly depressed 1962 reading of "House of the Risin' Sun," perhaps the Bob Dylan recording least likely to benefit from special effects, and then presented Dylan with the results (as, later in 1965, Wilson would do with an acoustic version of Simon and Garfunkel's "The Sounds of Silence," which became an enormous international hit), these were Dylan's first rock 'n' roll recordings. He had recorded with a band in 1962, for songs that were included on or omitted from *The Freewheelin' Bob Dylan,* including a prancing cover of "That's All Right," Elvis Presley's first single; Dylan's first single, from the same year, the unnoticed "Mixed Up Confusion," had guitars, bass, piano, drums, and a beat. But this was jug-band music; it didn't speak Chuck Berry's language, not to mention Little Richard's. Dylan's new sound on *Bringing It All Back Home* was a bid for Beatle territory, for pop success—and oddly, given what was to happen a few months later, no alarms were sounded. Despite a threatening jacket photo by Daniel Kramer, a tableau vivant that invited whoever was looking into a demimonde of expensive clothes and laudanum, where Robert Johnson traded songs with Lotte Lenya, a forgotten nineteenth-century politician gazed down from a mantel at Lyndon Johnson on the cover of *Time*, and an elegant woman in a red dress haughtily looked you in the eye as Dylan clutched a small gray cat as if it were his Doppelgänger, the new songs sounded, as a fan told Dylan in England that spring, "like you're just having a laugh."

The best laugh was the last song on the side. "Bob Dylan's 115th Dream" begins with a laugh, as a take opening with Dylan strumming his acoustic guitar stops short, and Tom Wilson breaks down in giggles, as if he's just pulled off a great practical joke. They start again: a single milky note from Bruce Langhorne's electric guitar tips the first words into the drums. The song was a kind of answer record to Chuck Berry's 1959 "Back in the U.S.A."—one of those rare works of pop art where, as with Richard Hamilton's 1956 collage *Just what is it that makes today's homes so different, so appealing?* you get the feeling that whatever irony might have been present as the artist began was burnt off by the fervor he or she brought to the work by the time it was finished. In Berry's case, he'd just returned from a tour of Australia. "Ooo-*bah*," chant the backing singers on the chorus, breathing real American air and letting it out. Berry is singing about freeways, hamburgers, jukeboxes. "It was a real thrill to get into my own Cadillac . . . and drive myself sixty miles per hour up I–55 to my own home," he wrote in his autobiography—not of returning from Australia in 1959, but of returning from Federal prison in 1963, where he'd been sent by a racist prosecutor on a trumped-up charge. There is a keen sense of the implacability and variety of American racism all through Berry's book; there is no irony in "Back in the U.S.A." and there was no irony in Bob Dylan's discovery of it.

The late San Francisco collage artist Jess once spoke of "the hermetic critique lockt up in art." The critique locked up in protest songs was not hermetic, and despite a rock 'n' roll sound "Bob Dylan's 115th Dream" was a protest song—though it was a protest song that made "Maggie's Farm" feel almost as sententious as "The Times They Are A-Changin'." A rewrite of the Bently Boys' 1929 pickin'-and-grinnin' sharecroppers' complaint "Down on Penny's Farm" and a precursor of Johnny Paycheck's 1977 "Take This Job and Shove It," "Maggie's Farm" was a protest song about factories, sweatshops, offices, jobs, chores, classrooms, and despite word-

play that would keep it on fans' lips for years, Dylan sounded
bored as he sang it.

He didn't sound bored in "Bob Dylan's 115th Dream."
Unlike "Maggie's Farm," "Who Killed Davey Moore?" "Masters of War," "Only a Pawn in Their Game," and many more,
if this was a protest song it was not rhetorical. When the
singer asked a question, he did not assume the answer would
be as plain to his listeners as it was to him. He didn't presume it would be plain at all—perhaps because like "Back in
the U.S.A." this protest song was also a celebration: a celebration of the failure of rational humanism in these United
States. Compared to the rock 'n' roll records Berry had made
ten years before, "Bob Dylan's 115 Dream" is primitive, all
trip stumble and fall, jangle and screech, with New York studio musicians, notably drummer Bobby Gregg and pianist
Paul Griffin, trying to keep up with Dylan, sometimes even
getting a step ahead, as in perfect dream logic a sailor casts
his eyes upon Fitzgerald's "fresh, green breast of the new
world."

He arrives on the *Mayflower*, which is also the *Pequod*:
"Boys, forget the whale," Captain Ahab shouts. For some reason, the place looks and sounds just like the United States in
1965.

"I think I'll call it America," the singer says as he kneels on
the beach. Captain Ahab—Dylan calls him *"Ay*-rab," no
doubt in tribute to Ray Stevens's 1962 hit "Ahab, the Arab,"
pronounced "Ay-rab"—is already writing deeds, planning to

"set up a fort and start buying the place with beads." Before he can do that, a cop shows up and arrests the entire crew for carrying harpoons.

The singer escapes—"Don't even ask me how," he says, this is all moving very fast, inside the shiny sound the band is making a dog is chasing its tail, the singer has a tale to tell and he's barely three steps into it. You can't tell if what's driving him forward is exasperation, amusement, disbelief, or the momentum of someone pushed off a cliff. Everywhere he goes, people turn him away, beat him up, steal his clothes. He dashes into a government building; the bureaucrat he encounters tells him to get lost. "You know, they refused Jesus, too," the singer says, as if the last thing he expects is for the line to get him any help. "You're not him," the bureaucrat says reasonably. The singer goes back to the street, which is now running backwards and upside down. "A pay phone was ringing," he says, "and it just about blew my mind/ When I picked it up and said hello, this foot came through the line." He seems surprised; by this time, the listener isn't. *Hey,* you say to the sailor, *it's a* phone. *What did you expect?*

Finally, the singer flees. He goes back to his ship, takes the parking ticket off the mast, weighs anchor. For the first time since the song began he lets a breath out easily. But the story isn't quite over. The singer gets out of the U.S.A. but the listener doesn't; the singer gets the last laugh. "When I was leavin' the bay," he tells you,

I saw three ships a-sailin'
They were all heading my way
I asked the captain what his name was
And how come he didn't drive a truck
He said his name was Columbus
I just said, "Good luck"

Despite this—"All my songs end with 'good luck,'" Dylan once said—the country in "Bob Dylan's 115th Dream" is at once a horror movie and a utopia, phantasmagoric and immediately recognizable, complete with protest marches, hot dogs, undertakers, transvestites, con artists, pimps, and Brotherhood crusades. It's supposed to sound crazy—or is it supposed to sound what it sounds like now and what it sounded like when it was made, which is completely realistic and utterly glamorous? Fun? A great adventure?

It's a protest song about a country that is ridiculous before it is anything else. It is, among other things, a rewrite of Ralph Ellison's 1952 novel *Invisible Man*, a comic version of the story Dylan would tell a few months later in "Like a Rolling Stone," and a picture of a life that hasn't changed—a common, modern story that doesn't make any more or less sense than it did when it was first told. Heard today, the song can seem more than anything a story about the modern market as a thing in itself, a song so complete it's less a song than a movie—a movie that could be shot in the center of any great city in the world, right now, with people bouncing back and forth as randomly as pinballs, everybody talking on cell phones, checking pagers, punching notebooks, some people talking into their wrists, into the Dick Tracy wristphones that fifty years after Chester Gould thought them up are finally on sale, everyone talking, nobody noticing anybody else because nobody has *time*, everybody trying desperately to use up time as fast as they can, because time is money, and there's nothing more thrilling to do with money than spend it. "Breathless," Dylan could have called the song; you don't want it to end. And that, for a protest song, is the best laugh of all. As with the state of the nation, caught up in a crisis it had yet to truly acknowledge, the arrival of the Beatles, and the call-and-response of the Top 40, "Bob Dylan's 115th Dream" was a stage for "Like a Rolling Stone," a performance that would take in all those things, and send them back transformed.

There was no laughter on the other side of the album. There, except for "Mr. Tambourine Man" and "It's All Over Now, Baby Blue," where single backing instruments were so subtle they seemed more like emanations from the songs than pieces added to them, this was Bob Dylan as he had always been, alone, with his guitar and harmonica. The side comprised four long songs, all of which promised they would never get near Top 40 radio—and they were so self-evidently full of meaning, so striking, so important, so elegant and so beautiful that their quiet drowned out the noise of the songs on the other side. Bob Dylan may have meant to draw a line, but it was in a furrow already plowed, and flowers grew over it. The faster he moved, the more his trap held.

PART TWO

CHAPTER FOUR

San Jose Idol

Speaking with Bob Dylan—do you say "Dillon" or "Die-lan"?

Oh, I say "Dillon" ... "Die-lan" ...I say anything you say, really.

Did you take it from the Welsh poet?

No—that's, I guess we could say, a rumor, made up by people who like to simplify things ...

What particular song do you remember as being a breakthrough for you? Was it "Blowing in the Wind"?

No, no, it was—do you mean the most honest and straight thing which I thought I ever put across? That reached popularity, you mean. There's been a few—there's been a few. "Blowin' in the Wind" was to a degree, but I was just a *kid*. I didn't know anything about anything, at that point. I just wrote that, and—that was it, really. Ah—"Mr. Tambourine Man." I was very close to that song. I kept if off my third album, just because I felt too close to it, to put it on.

If you're talking about what breakthrough is for me, I would have to say, speaking totally, "Like a Rolling Stone."

I wrote that after I had *quit.* I'd literally quit, singing and playing—I found myself writing this song, this story, this long piece of vomit, twenty pages long, and out of it I took "Like a Rolling Stone" and made it as a single. And I'd never written anything like that before and it suddenly came to me that this is what I should do.

Nobody had ever done that before. A lot of people— Anybody can write . . . a lot of the things I used to write, I just wrote 'em first because nobody else could think of writing them. But that's only because I was hungry. But I've never met anybody, or heard anything—I hear a lot—I'm not saying it's *better* than anything else, I'm saying that I think—I think "Like a Rolling Stone" is definitely the thing which I do. After writing that I wasn't interested in writing a novel, or a play. I just had too much, I want to write *songs.* Because it was a whole new category. I mean, nobody's ever really written *songs* before, really.

—Bob Dylan interviewed by Marvin Bronstein, CCBC, Montreal, 20 February 1966

That night, every time he named the song he pressed down just slightly on the second-to-last word, so that it almost came out "Like a *Rolling* Stone." And it wasn't the song, it was the sound.

In 1884, Mrs. Sarah L. Winchester, the recently widowed wife of Oliver Winchester, the inventor of the Winchester Repeating Rifle—"The Gun that Won the West," as the 1873 model was called, though Bill Cody simply named his "The Boss"—was told by a spiritualist that as long as she continued building her house in San Jose, California, she would never die. Crews of carpenters, plumbers, masons, and painters were on the property the next day. For the next thirty-eight years, as the Winchester mansion expanded to 160 rooms, with stairways that led to ceilings and windows opening onto walls, they worked without cease—until 1922, when the wrong person must have taken a break at the wrong time.

Eighty-one years after Mrs. Winchester's death, in June 2003, the San Francisco Classic Rock station KFOG set up a broadcast in Mrs. Winchester's house—by then the Winchester Mystery House, where, it used to be said, the ghosts of dead Indians hung in the air. The station was there to host a local version of the hit television show *American Idol*: "San Jose Idol," in which members of the studio audience would sing Bob Dylan songs in the hopes of winning tickets to his upcoming show at Konocti Harbor, a California resort featuring performers who appeal to a redundant demographic—as opposed to the contestants on *American Idol* itself, who sing florid power ballads and Mariah Carey "Endless Love" imitations in hopes of winning a record contract and sales to the millions who, the idea is, will in turn copy the contestants' received inflections and grimaces in hopes of someday becoming winners themselves. Thus in San Jose men and women were stepping up to the microphone to essay the most lugubrious versions imaginable of the likes of "All Along the Watchtower" or "Just Like a Woman"—moronically drawing out the vowels, of course. "That's the most beautiful thing I've ever heard!" cooed the Paula Abdul stand-in judge. "That's horrible and you're too fat!" barked the Simon Cowell.

You listen and you think, here's the real Bob Dylan, alive in the public imagination: the world's most beloved cliché, or anyway the most obvious. Were the winners of this contest really going to keep the tickets they won? If this is who Bob Dylan is to the people on this show, why would they want to see him? Why would anyone?

This is the premise of *Masked and Anonymous*, a movie released that same summer, directed by Larry Charles, written by Bob Dylan, and starring Dylan as Jack Fate, a semilegendary, all-but-forgotten singer: people remember they're supposed to remember him, but they don't remember why. They are citizens of a country that barely remembers itself: the U.S.A. here reduced to a rotting Los Angeles. Most of the people who used to run the country, or own it—that is, white people—have fled or disappeared. Those who remain still speak and move as if they expect others to respect what they say or get out of the way, but nobody does. There are no more Americans. The Third World—Jamaicans, Africans, Mexicans, Arabs, Chechens, Serbs, refugees, thugs, killers, and extortionists of every kind—has colonized the First.

These are not the Statue of Liberty's huddled masses, yearning to breathe free; they're looters.

In a nation that is breaking up in a civil war between "rebels," "counterrevolutionaries," and a government that seems to consist principally of posters of a dying president (in his smudgy white and gold military uniform, a cross between Saddam Hussein and Juan Perón), Jack Fate has been released from prison to play a "benefit concert," because Sting, Bruce Springsteen, Billy Joel, and Paul McCartney have already said no. It's a scam for the promoter, Sweetheart, played by John Goodman in an ugly beard and a grimy blue tuxedo jacket, who plans to skim the money, and a board of gangsters who claim to represent the president and want to "aid the true victims of the revolution." Or skim the money.

The film moves to pick up Jack Fate from the prison where he's been held for years on charges that are never described—and as it does so it swiftly carries the viewer through an America that has been boiled down to greed and violent death, a montage of urban massacres and broken streets crowded with human wreckage. The characters who emerge or merely appear to disappear—Val Kilmer as a shepherd in a parking lot, a blowsy Jessica Lange as an even more cynical version of Goodman's promoter, clean-cut Luke Wilson as an old Jack Fate sidekick, or bodyguard—together make up a caricature of Bob Dylan's, or Jack Fate's, original audience: washed-up, self-loathing, culturally narcissistic middle-aged white people trying to find something better to do than sing Townes van Zandt's "Waiting Around to Die," or talk about how Townes van Zandt died.

Throughout the film, all of the music, save for the versions of "Dixie" and the folk song "Diamond Joe" that Fate plays with Simple Twist of Fate—announced by Sweetheart as "the best and only Jack Fate tribute band!"—is Dylan's: his own original recordings, deeply empathetic transformations of his songs by others ("My Back Pages" by the Magokoro Brothers, in Japanese, "Most of the Time" by the Swedish singer Sophie Zelmani, "If You See Her, Say Hello" by Francesco de Gregori, in Italian), and performances that occur as part of the action, most stunningly when, during a Jack Fate rehearsal for the big concert, a white woman with a cast on her arm and a tattoo on her leg is brought in with her daughter, a black girl of about eight or nine. "Mrs. Brown, you've got a lovely daughter," someone says, and explains to Fate that, out of a devotion that has crossed from the mere schizophrenia of fandom to outright child abuse, the woman has taught, or forced, the girl to memorize every one of his songs. She is commanded to sing—and produces a lovely, too-perfect, word-for-word a cappella rendition of "The Times They Are A-Changin'." The girl plainly has no idea what she is singing or why; in her own English she is singing in a foreign language.

The song summons a far-off, forgotten time that no longer makes sense. It's a call to action in a country that no longer exists. "Senators, Congressmen, please heed the call/ Don't stand in the doorway, don't block up the hall," the girl sings, as Jack Fate, or Bob Dylan, sang in 1963, but there is no longer any Senate or House of Representatives: hustlers run three-card monte games in the Capitol doorways, crack fiends sleep in the halls. It's a chilling moment, as Jack Fate listens and turns away and the girl and her mother are escorted out without even a thank you or a smile, as if this is the last thing Jack Fate wants to be reminded of—that once he wrote such things, that once people believed them, that he believed them, or that he once pretended to believe them.

As a fantasy of Bob Dylan, Jack Fate—walking carefully, as if his boots are stilts, a thin man who looks like Vincent Price, wears a Little Richard moustache, dresses like Hank Williams, and squints like Clint Eastwood—talks to the ghost of a long-dead blackface minstrel, played by an unrecognizable Ed Harris with huge white lips painted onto his burnt-cork face. On a bus, he listens to a crazed ex-revolutionary played by Giovanni Ribisi, who after explaining who's on what side and which side is which runs out of the bus to try to stop guerrilla fighters who blow him to pieces. He does not talk or listen to Tom Friend, played by Jeff Bridges as a fantasy of every journalist of the last forty years who tried to get an interview with Bob Dylan. Dispatched by a muckraking editor to dig up the story behind the phony benefit concert, Bridges has a list of questions—and he's so convulsed by his own theories of what it all means, the hope of the sixties, the corruption of the present, the possibility that maybe the concert *will* save the world, his obsession with Fate's career, his own career, or simply the sound of his own voice (*he's* the real Jack Fate, he seems to be saying, or would be if there were any justice in this world) that Fate couldn't get a word in even if he wanted to.

In the early nineties, I was sent a proposal and a pilot video for a TV series on great rock festivals. The premise was almost scary in its insistence on the eternal primacy of those born after World War II and before Vietnam: the show would start with the greatest concert of all time—Woodstock, the instantly storied 1969 "Gathering of the Tribes"—and then move on through a series of only slightly less storied gatherings, most involving at least one dead hero those not dead could talk about ("He was the nicest person you could ever meet" "She had her demons, but she was the nicest person you could ever meet"). Each segment would end with its host, a current movie or music star, speaking the same line, the catchphrase of the whole series: "You shoulda been there, man." The whole point was to stress that the world is made up of two different kinds of people, those who'd been there, and those who hadn't—and the host for the Woodstock episode, standing under a bright sun in the field where the stage once was, saying "You shoulda been there, man" with cheerleader condescension, was Jeff Bridges.

Thus here he is again in *Masked and Anonymous*, shaggier, heavier, looking as if he hasn't slept for the ten years between

the day he shot the pilot and the reemergence of Jack Fate
but with exactly the same attitude, now pumped up as pure
mania. He's following Fate as they walk through the old
vaudeville theater where the benefit concert is going to take
place. (Is that how the movie will end? Cheers, calls for an
encore that never comes, "Jack Fate has left the building," and
then a cut to Tom Friend, on the late news, summing it all up,
"You shoulda been there, man"?) The hulking Friend looms
over Fate like a thunderhead, and he goes off.

What about the Mothers of Invention, Jack—Zappa. Now there's a
guy, he wouldn't take no for an answer. He did that whole movie,
Uncle Meat, sixteen hours long, unedited. He let it all hang out,
didn't he? What about you? Do you ever let it all hang out? You
know the singer in the group the Bee Gees, he sounds a lot like, ah,
Gene Pitney! Doesn't he? "Town without Pity." You remember that,
Jack? That place where they'd lock you up for something you
haven't even thought about doing yet? It's a pretty lonesome world
... What about Hendrix? Remember Hendrix at Woodstock? I'm
just curious, you weren't there, were you? You weren't at Woodstock, weren't up there with Hendrix. Why? Where were you? You
shoulda seen Hendrix, man. He was—all business. Didn't mix business with pleasure. And playing "The Star-Spangled Banner,"
through two lousy speakers to half a million people in the mud?
Oooo! What a cry that was! Cry forlorn. Man, it was a desperate
cry of freedom up there with that screaming guitar. What was he
sayin', Jack? That "Star-Spangled Banner" trip. Now, what was that

all about, huh? Revolution? I don't think so. You could hear—*tears*, in every note he played, sayin', love me. *Love me.* I'm not a *traitor*— I'm a native son! He took the—glorious anthem, he dropped drug bombs on it. You could hear that cry around the world, saying, Hey! *I'm an American citizen!* He was calling out to his forefathers, the Pilgrims, the Pilgrims! They didn't need any stinking passports, did they? Hmmm? Hendrix, Jack, well—he was the last man standing. Pride and honor, right? That's what it's all about. But they didn't hear him. One sad cry of pain. In a town without pity.

Jack Fate listens stonefaced and turns away. But what Jimi Hendrix did with the National Anthem at Woodstock—in just under four minutes twisting and shredding it with feedback, scattering the pieces all over the stage and then drawing them back, reassembling them into a Frankenstein monster of a nation, then finally letting the song emerge in its whole body, the hateful noise and furious love of Hendrix's music now draped over the song like a wedding suit covered in dirt—is what is happening with Fate's own music, Bob Dylan's music, everywhere in the film. It's a music of transformations, gathering its greatest force with "Come una Pietra Scalciata," a 1998 recording by Articolo 31, an Italian hip-hop group made up of J. Ax and DJ Jad: that is, with "Like a Rolling Stone."

This strange, utterly displacing performance is reaching back to "Like a Rolling Stone" as it appeared in 1965, reaching back through the confusion of events that has by the near-future of the film negated the first shape of the song, back through the time that has dimmed it, the thousands of other songs that took its place on the charts, the world it changed, the world that changed around it, that left it behind at a fork in the road—maybe that fabled fork in the American road with two signs, "THIS WAY TO TEXAS," "THIS WAY TO ARKANSAS," with, as the story goes, everyone who could read proceeding to Texas, and everyone else ending up in Arkansas. So the song goes to Arkansas, in the folk iconography of the story of the signs to nowhere. For the Italians who are now claiming the song as if it were itself a forefather, a founding father, a Jefferson, a Garibaldi, nothing remains but a distant, inherited memory of what the song once meant. But they don't play it as a memory. What their performance affirms, what it seizes as a birthright that passes the song from the one who once sang it to the people speaking it now, is precisely that confusion of events, less "Like a Rolling Stone" as it was found than "Like a Rolling Stone" as it was lost.

With "Come una Pietra Scalciata," even Dylan himself is a kind of haunt. The record is in fact a cover of a cover—a cover of the 1993 cover of "Like a Rolling Stone" by the enigmatic white hip-hop group the Mystery Tramps.*

---

* Their fourth Google entry turns up not the band but "The thesis of *Coup d'E-tat in America* suggested that Watergate conspirator and longtime CIA spook E. Howard Hunt was one of the three mystery tramps renowned in Kennedy assassination lore." Given that the tramps, "photographed in the vicinity of the grassy knoll," were "picked up by the Dallas police and then released without any record of arrest," maybe they *are* the band.

In both the four-minute-thirty-second "Radio Mix" and
the six-minute-twenty-six-second "1-800-Mix," the Mystery
Tramps open with a sample of the original fanfare: distant,
thin, and undeniable, like the vision of Shangri-La Ronald
Colman can't get out of his head. Over a conventional hip-
hop drum and bass track, there's a thick, crass, tiresomely
knowing male lead singer, instantly answered by an auto-
matic female chorus. There's scratching, and then a sample
of Bob Dylan: "How does it feel?" "Check it out," says the
leader, sounding as if he wants to sell you dope. "This a story
about a girl who goes from riches to rags, and it's a drag, so
check it *ouuuuuut.*" It's the most reductive story in the song:
"a put-down," as Jon Landau described it in 1968, full of
"self-righteousness, its willingness to judge others without
judging oneself"; an example of "sixties songwriters" refusing
"women any middle ground between the pedestal and the
gutter," as Charles Shaar Murray wrote in 1989, a song
"sneeringly and contemptuously sung to a spoiled rich girl,"
with "the reactionary stagnation of the social order . . . per-
sonified as female"; "a view of the Socialite life of the Big
Apple," as C. P. Lee wrote in 1998, if not "another song
about" the Warhol actress Edie Sedgwick. "Even now," Dave
Marsh wrote in 1989, "it still seems strange that the record is
so long because in real life, diatribes are never allowed to
last this long: somebody interrupts." The Mystery Tramp
singer can't wait to push the buttons. "How does it feel? I
really want to know," he says, but he already knows. There's

only one real hint of the bad news the leader insists the song is about but never offers: when he chants "Nobody ever taught you how to live out on the street," you hear a car honk. Something in the timing of the way it comes in, the abruptness of the horn, as if the driver is both angry and shocked, lets you see who he's honking at: someone wandering in traffic, oblivious, confused, someone who has given up.

Right at the beginning of the first chorus, there's a cut-in of a girl in the bloom of youth: "Spare change?" she says. "Spare change, anybody?" Her voice is so clear and untroubled, so much the girl in the first panel of Mick Brownfield's comic strip version of the song, that you don't believe her for a moment. When the singer gets to the third verse, which for the Mystery Tramps is also the last verse, to "After he took from you everything that he could steal," the girl is back, as if from a sitcom: "Hey! Where's my stuff?" The recurrent Dylan sample, "How does it feel?" is plaintive and small, Midwestern, heard as if from across the country, and, along with the girl on the street, the only source of soul in the piece. You hear Dylan calling out to her—he's the one who really wants to know.

The shorter version ends with the girl buried in a fade, barely audible: "What is this? Can you help me?" That will be the heart of the long mix. There's that fanfare again, but speeded up and tinny, with a heavier rhythm on top of it, and then a second male voice, a more secretive voice: "Yeah, can you dig it?" It's a hipster's tone, an old man's gravel in the throat: the Mystery Tramp. And then the girl whose last words were almost lost at the end of the first version comes through all too clearly, in a panic: "What is this? Can you help me out? Where am I, what's going on— This isn't cool." She is trapped in the song as if she were locked in a closet. "Heh, heh, heh," says the Mystery Tramp.

The sneer Charles Shaar Murray heard when Bob Dylan sang the song, that the Mystery Tramps heard, is altogether gone when Articolo 31 takes up the Mystery Tramps' arrangement five years later.

There is a distorted, nasal, Dylan-like voice: "I got, I got something to *tell* you," and instantly you are plunged into darkness. Like the girl in the Mystery Tramps' "1-800" version, you don't know where you are. There is the original fanfare, sounding like the trumpets of Jubilee—and then a harsh but leveled rap, relentlessly chasing what seem like thousands of words.

Articolo 31's "Come una Pietra Scalciata" is a rewrite of "Like a Rolling Stone," following Dylan's themes, only three verses in four and a half minutes, but in terms of its Italian word count at least four and a half times as long as Dylan's long song. It's a flood of words, with the first verse run over a chopped, pulled-back sample of the original fanfare behind a slow hip-hop rhythm track, then a new organ track. A repeated sample of the lilting piano from Dylan's original recording is the dominant instrumental sound, all loose notes, like pieces flying off a machine in motion. The song is shattered, but it never loses its body, reconstituting itself as if each fragment carries a genetic code. And then Dylan, with the same faraway sample of "How does it feel?" that the Mystery Tramps used, but this time the female singers for the chorus are warm, present, full of desire. They are actors, not a sound effect; as Dylan calls out they answer him. This is how it feels—complete, knowledgeable, strong, and Dylan continues as they do, the spectral singer and the flesh-and-blood women now answering each other line by line, neither side surrendering anything.

Both ride the chorus like a horse. As the women throw every line that comes from Dylan in English back to him in Italian, as if there's nothing he can tell them they don't already know, you can hear him singing directly to them, as if they were always the subject of the song, the audience it sought. It's as if he means to tell them, with more passion than his voice, heard as it was recorded in 1965, has ever carried before, that there is something they don't know, something they cannot know, because like the language in which he made the song it has been forgotten. The feeling generated by "Come una Pietra Scalciata" is finally that the Dylan captured in the recording is not asking how it feels but what it means—and you can hear the women singing directly to him, as if the song is now as much theirs as his. He is questioning; they are deliberate. For them the chorus is a staircase and each word is a stair.

How does it feel?

Dimmi comme ci sente

To be on your own?

A stare sempre da sola

With no direction home?

Nè direzione nè casa

A second rapper comes in for the second verse, moving faster than the first, over a more cut-up, stop-and-start sample from the original, moving faster over the slower, jerking rhythm. Then the chorus returns—with familiarity, with repetition, even more powerful, even more alive—and then the first rapper, back to take the third and last verse, as if he can't believe how many words there are left, as if this is a chance to say everything he's ever wanted to say, and have it validated by the way Bob Dylan will answer him—"How does it feel?"—and the way he will answer back: *"e dimmi come ci si sente ora che devi sudarti i beni materiali vedi che hai poco spazio per i problemi esistenziali . . ."*

All sense of a put-down, of a sneer, has been erased as if it never was—if it ever was. ("Why does everybody say of something like 'Like a Rolling Stone,'" Dylan asked Robert Shelton in 1965, "'That Dylan . . . is that all he can do, put down people? I've never put anybody down in a song, man.'") In the few moments of the song that play on the soundtrack of Dylan's film—the fanfare, the first rap, the first chorus—it comes through whole, moving across the scenes of social collapse, of America as a plague, like a call to arms. It's thrilling; it's confusing. In this blasted version of the U.S.A. as what you see and what you hear refuse to come together, the song asks not how a new life feels, but why what is now so plainly an affirmation of freedom, of a world to win, has persisted in any form at all. It's as if you're hearing a distorted radio signal from a station that went out of business years ago, or—with the body of the song now cut up and reassembled with pieces of bodies of people not born when the song was first heard— as if the true precursor of "Like a Rolling Stone" is not Ritchie Valens's "La Bamba" but the Drifters' "There Goes My Baby," from 1959, with its sound of two or three or four different stations cutting in and out of the same band, the classical station, the R&B station, the Top 40 station, the ether, a mistake that will leave your life forever incomplete, because you will never hear it again, because you will never be sure you heard it at all.

CHAPTER FIVE

Once Upon a Time

The song is a sound, but before that it is a story. But it's not one story. "I have the audacity to *play* 'Like a Rolling Stone' in my show, just about every night," the country singer Rodney Crowell said in 2004. "I did it as a lark, to show off to some of the guys in my band that I knew all the words. But I was immediately struck by the audience response to the song. From six-year-olds to seventy-year-olds—*they all know the chorus to that song.* I couldn't put it away; every night, it's a unifying thing. I think it's somehow part of the fabric of our culture."

"This is about growing up, this is about discovering what's going on around you, realizing that life isn't all you've been told," Jann Wenner said that same year; thirty-seven years before, in 1967, he had named his magazine *Rolling Stone* because, as he explained in the first issue, "Muddy Waters took the name for a song he wrote; the Rolling Stones took their name from Muddy's song, and 'Like a Rolling Stone' was the title of Bob Dylan's first rock and roll record."

He's throwing it at you in the verse: here's your problem. Here's what's happened. So now you're without a home, you're on your own, complete unknown, like a rolling stone. That's a liberating thing. This *is* a song about liberation. About being liberated from your old hang-ups, and your old knowledge, and the fear, the frightening part of facing that, particularly when he gets to scrounging for your next meal—the worst thing that happens to you. Or, *"Do you want to make a deal"*—there's a lot of *fear* in that, in the line, in the lyric, in the melody.

"Once upon a time you dressed so fine"—I don't see it as being about a rich person who falls apart, I see it as being about a *comfortable* individual, or a comfortable society, suddenly discovering what's going on. Vietnam—the society we're taught about, and you realize, as you become aware, drug aware, socially aware, the disaster of the commercial society.

The key line is, "You've got no secrets to conceal." Everything has been stripped away. You're on your own, you're free now. You've gone through all these levels of experience—you fell, someone you believed in robbed you blind, took everything he could steal, and finally, it's all been taken away. You're so helpless, and now you've got *nothing* left. And you're invisible—you've got no secrets—that's so liberating. You've nothing to fear anymore. It's

useless to hide any of that shit. *You're a free man.* That to me is the
message. You know: "Songs of Innocence and Experience."

I always thought it was my story, in a certain sense. *I* used to go
to the finest schools. Nobody ever taught you how to live out on
the street. So, to me, coming from private schools, and my background, being a preppy, ending up at Berkeley, and all of a sudden,
taking drugs, things change, you're no longer in a private school,
all of a sudden you're running around with Ken Kesey, Hell's
Angels, and drug dealers—and one of *them's* the Mystery Tramp. At
some Acid Test, and some weirdo comes up to you, with a beard, a
top hat—you stare into the vacuum of his eyes, and ask him, do
you want to make a deal. That *happened* to me. *Too* many times.

In 1978, in *Jimi Hendrix: Voodoo Child of the Aquarian Age,*
David Henderson made it Jimi Hendrix's story. The finest
writing there is on "Like a Rolling Stone" is Henderson on
the performance of the song at the Monterey Pop Festival in
1967 by the Jimi Hendrix Experience, Hendrix's first band. It
was a great stomp, as much a fan's tribute as a master's appro-
priation: "Yes, I know I missed a verse, don't worry," Hendrix
says after skipping from the second to the fourth. Huge
chords ride over the beginning of each verse like rain clouds;
the tune is taken very slowly, with Hendrix's thick, street-talk
drawl sounding nothing at all like Dylan's Midwestern dust
storm. Laughter erupts all over the song: "Hey, baby—would
you like to, ah, ah, make a *deeeallllllll?*" But for the six minutes
Hendrix is playing, across five pages Henderson all but leaves

the song on the stage and enters Hendrix's mind as he plays. Now "Like a Rolling Stone" is about Hendrix's childhood in Seattle, where as a schoolboy he attended an Elvis Presley show at the Rainiers minor-league baseball park, when Elvis asked all present to rise for the National Anthem and then plunged into "Hound Dog"; his years as a journeyman on the Chitlin' Circuit; his tours with Joey Dee and the Starlighters of "Peppermint Twist" fame; his life in Harlem—an odyssey. Henderson turns himself into Hendrix's shade, as if in these pages of fiction he was watching from across the street, writing it down as it happened.

"Once upon a time you dressed so fine . . ." Right there in that moment Jimi saw himself as he had lived in America. Yeah, he had been the fine-dressing R&B entertainer, and then suffered what many of his friends at the time thought was a great fall. Hanging out in the Village with all those beatniks and hippies. Taking all that speed for energy and to fend off starvation. The slick veneer front of the R&B musician destroyed for him in the Village. Disdain from his friends "uptown"—"he's looking scruffy and acting crazy."

He saw himself walking MacDougal Street hearing the song, and every time always so amazed at how it hit so close to home. "Like a Rolling Stone" seemed to come forth from every window, every bar. Once he had walked clear across the Village to the East Village, and stopped in a bar called The Annex on Tenth Street and Avenue B. Out of the sodden, snow-encrusted streets, dark and severe and utterly desolate, he walked into the slit-windowed one-room Annex where a great swell of music greeted him, and the entire bar was singing along. The jukebox was turned up to full volume. The place was dark but packed, and they were all singing "...Rolling Stone" jubilantly, as if it were the National Anthem.

And then Henderson takes Hendrix deeper into a new life, into his first hesitant performances in tiny clubs, as he found his way to "the odd folk and blues records so treasured by so many in the Village," as his attempts to play Bob Dylan records for his Harlem friends were met with scorn and disgust, as he stood with the other hustlers on Forty-second Street, "waiting for some stranger to give them a nod." As Hendrix plays the song, Henderson as Hendrix reverses its perspective, taking it away from Dylan's subject, the *you* who "used to laugh about/ Everybody that was hanging out," and giving the song over to the nameless people hiding in the song's alleys and doorways, people like Hendrix, scuffling downtown: "They had laughed at him." "It was a song that only Dylan could sing—until now," Henderson writes, but it's he who is singing it. It's he who has passed it on. As Henderson tells it, "Like a Rolling Stone" is not a story of liberation, it is an epic.*

---

* "I think Jimi's gonna be remembered for centuries, just like people like Leadbelly and Lightnin' Hopkins," the late John Phillips, one of the organizers of the Monterey Pop Festival, said in 1992, then placing Hendrix in an America so alluring and mysterious that it changed Hendrix's story once again, recasting his whole brief career as a dare, or a race against an opponent Phillips didn't name, opening up a tale yet to be told: "He's really a folk hero, another John Henry."

CHAPTER SIX

In the Air

As songwriting, what's different about "Like a Rolling Stone" is all in its first four words. There may not be another pop song or a folk song that begins with "Once upon a time . . ."—that in a stroke takes the listener into a fairy tale, off the radio you're listening to in your car or on the record player in your house, suddenly demanding that all the paltry incidents in the song and all the impoverished incidents in your own life that the song reveals as you listen now be understood as a part of a myth: part of a story far greater than the person singing or the person listening, a story that was present before they were and that will remain when they're gone. But the entry into the realm of fairy tale, of dragons and sorcerers, knights and maidens, of princes traveling the kingdom disguised as peasants and girls banished from their

homes roaming the land disguised as boys, would mean nothing if the singer's feet were on the ground.

There is that stick coming down hard on the drum and
the foot hitting the kick drum at the same time, this particular rifle going off not in the third act but as the curtain goes
up. "The first time I heard Bob Dylan," Bruce Springsteen said
in 1989, inducting Dylan into the Rock and Roll Hall of
Fame, "I was in the car with my mother listening to WMCA,
and on came that snare shot that sounded like somebody'd
kicked open the door to your mind." Many other recordings
have opened with the same formal device, a single drum
beat—"From a Buick 6," on *Highway 61 Revisited*, the album
"Like a Rolling Stone" leads off, is one—but on no other
record does the sound, or the act, so call attention to itself, as
an absolute announcement that something new has begun.*

Then for an expanding instant there is nothing. The first
sound is so stark and surprising, every time you hear it, that
the empty split-second that follows calls up the image of a

---

* As a way to start a song, this has always struck me as completely singular—
not, it's plain, because it is singular, but because the drama created by the isolation of the sound for "Like a Rolling Stone," perhaps the echo that surrounds
it, for me erased all analogues. "Do you remember how that came about?" I
asked Al Kooper. "It's a very common situation," he said. "Somebody counts
off, and somebody plays a lead-in. It's a very common thing to play a drum fill
on one of the first bars. He [drummer Bobby Gregg] could have gone, *one, two,
three—chickaboom;* there's a million things you could do. He just chose to do
that. It's the *four* of the bar before it starts. *One, two, three, FOUR!* And there you
go." Kooper then offered a list of thirty records that begin the same way,
including the Impressions' 1963 "It's All Right," Richard Thompson's 1985

house tumbling over a cliff; it calls up a void. Even before "Once upon a time," it's the first suggestion of what Dylan meant when, on that night in Montreal when he was plainly too tired to bait an interviewer so uninterested in his assignment he hadn't even bothered to learn how to pronounce his subject's name, he cared enough about "Like a Rolling Stone" to seriously insist that no one had written songs before—that no one had ever tried to make as much of a song, to altogether open the territory it might claim, to make a song a story, and a sound, but also the Oklahoma Land Rush.

That first shot will be repeated throughout the performance, on Dylan's own electric rhythm guitar, as for every other measure a hard, percussive snap seals a phrase, cuts off one line of the story and challenges the moment to produce another. That first announcement is brought inside the sound, so that it becomes a signpost, reappearing every other step of the way: a mark of how far the story has gone, which is to say a mark of how much ground that can never be

---

[continued] "When the Spell Is Broken," the Dixie Chicks' 2000 "Goodbye Earl," the Beach Boys' kabbalistically obscure 1964 "Pom Pom Playgirl," and the Ronettes' 1963 "Sleigh Ride." Jon Langford, of the Mekons, noted the Mekons' own 1986 cover of Patsy Cline's "Sweet Dreams," where the effect is so similar it qualifies as a cover of "Like a Rolling Stone." Dave Marsh offered the Beatles' 1964 "Any Time at All": "It has the drum beat opening, and it is very close in effect; in fact, Ringo does the drum beat opening at the top of the record *and* at the top of every chorus. It's got that gunshot effect—not quick and sharp as on 'Like a Rolling Stone,' more duration, like a real gunshot." I am sticking to my guns. There is nothing like it.

recovered has been left behind. The silence, too, is repeated, in breaks in the sound too brief to measure but that in their affective force can seem enormous: the entire ensemble rising up and then stopping at the top of a surge, just after the first "How does it feel" of the final chorus, as if the song itself has to pause to catch its breath for the final chase; Dylan himself, in the time it takes the last word of the song to leave his mouth and his mouth to reach the harmonica on the rack on his chest for the slashing phrase that seals the end of the song as fiercely as the stick on the snare opened it. In these moments of suspension there is a kind of ghost, the phantom of a comforting past, where everything remains the same. In the maelstrom of the performance itself, in each step forward on the fairy-tale road, where when you look forward you see mountains too high to climb and when you look back you see nothing, it is the sense that you could take it all back, that you could retrace your steps, that you could go home, that it's not too late.

As a sound the record is like a cave. You enter it in the dark; what light there is flickers off the walls in patterns that, as you watch, seem almost in rhythm. You begin to feel that you can tell just what flash will follow from the one before it. But the longer you look, the more you see, and the less fixed anything is. The flickers turn into shadows, and the movement the shadows make can never be anticipated. Suddenly the dark, the light, and the shadows are all speaking to you, each demanding your attention. You can't look in all directions at once but you feel you must. The room begins to whirl; you try to focus on a single element, to make it repeat itself, to follow it, but you are instantly distracted by something else.

This is what happens in "Like a Rolling Stone." The sound is so rich the song never plays the same way twice. You can know that, for you, a certain word, a certain partial sound deep within the whole sound, is what you want; you can steel yourself to push everything else in the song away in anticipation of that part of the song you want. It never works. You lie in wait, to ambush the moment; you find that as you do another moment has sneaked up behind you and ambushed you instead. Without a chorus the song would truly be a flood, not the flood of words of "Come una Pietra Scalciata" but a flood that sweeps up everything before it—and yet as the song is actually sung and played, the chorus, formally the most determined, repeating element in the song, is the most unstable element of all.

There are drums, piano, organ, bass guitar, rhythm guitar, lead guitar, tambourine, and a voice. Though one instrument may catch you up, and you may decide to follow it, to attend only to the story it tells—the organ is pursuing the story of a road that forks every time you turn your head, the guitar is offering a fable about a seeker who only moves in circles, the singer is embellishing his fairy tale about the child lost in the forest—every instrument shoots out a line that leads to another instrument, the organ to the guitar, the guitar to the voice, the voice to the drums, until nothing is discrete and each instrument is a passageway. You cannot make anything hold still.

Because the song never plays the same way twice—because whenever you hear the song you are not quite hearing a song you have heard before—it cannot carry nostalgia. Unlike any other Bob Dylan recording that might be included on *Golden Protest*, the next time you hear "Like a Rolling Stone" is also the first time. That first drum shot is what seals it: when the stick hits the skin, even as a house tumbles forward, the past is jettisoned like a missile dumping its first stage. In that moment there is no past to refer to—especially the past you yourself might mean to bring to the song.

I saw this happen once, as if it were a play. It was about eleven in the morning in Lahaina, on Maui, in 1981, in a place called Longhi's, a restaurant made of blonde wood and ceiling fans. There were ferns. People were talking quietly; even small children were lolling in the heat. Everything seemed to move very slowly. There was a radio playing tunes from a local FM station, but it was almost impossible to focus on what they were. Then "Like a Rolling Stone" came on, and once again, as in the summer of 1965, sixteen years gone, with "Like a Rolling Stone" supposedly safely filed away in everyone's memory, the song interrupted what was going on: in this case, nothing. As if a note were being passed from one table to another, people raised their heads from their pineapple and Bloody Mary breakfasts; conversations fell away. People were moving their feet, and looking toward the radio as if it might get up and walk. It was a stunning moment: proof that "Like a Rolling Stone" cannot be used as Muzak. When the song was over, it was like the air had gone out of the room.

In early rock 'n' roll—in the Drifters' 1953 "Money Honey," Elvis Presley's 1956 "Hound Dog," Chuck Berry's "Johnny B. Goode" and Dion and the Belmonts' "I Wonder Why," both from 1958—you can hear the reach for the total sound that hovers in "Like a Rolling Stone." Sometimes the reach almost is the sound, as with the insensate, nearly a cappella last verse of Little Richard's 1956 "Ready Teddy," where he seems less a singer than a medium for some nameless god. Or in the preternaturally fast, perfectly balanced leaps that kick off "Johnny B. Goode" and "I Wonder Why." In the first it's six seconds of a guitar answered by a single downbeat combination on the drums, in the second it's a downpour of doo-wops, bassman Carlo Mastrangelo's *did-did did-it did-did-da-did-it*s before the leader comes in, for thirteen seconds a field for the other Belmonts to turn backflips into eternity. But "Money Honey" is probably the template. Of all the many first rock 'n' roll records it is the most unfettered, and it wasn't just a reach. At least for an instant you can feel the prize in its grasp.

The Drifters came about when in the spring of 1953 lead singer Clyde McPhatter was kicked out of the Dominoes, a hit rhythm and blues vocal group. Ahmet Ertegun of the young Atlantic label put McPhatter together with the four-man Thrasher Wonders and gave them all a new name. With the Dominoes, on angelic performances of "Close the Door," "When the Swallows Come Back to Capistrano," and "Don't Leave Me This Way," McPhatter's high tenor was the voice of the ineffable, tugging at your sleeve. As a Drifter he was a dynamo unlike anything pop music had seen before, but it was all over by 1954, when McPhatter received his draft notice. When he returned he never really found his music again. He died a forgotten drunk in 1972; he was thirty-nine. But in his one year of greatness he came out of himself. He ran wild with his own songs, with songs by Atlantic's musical director Jesse Stone—or for that matter Irving Berlin. As you listen now, a new man appears before you when McPhatter sings "Honey Love," "Such a Night," or "Let the Boogie Woogie Roll"; a story tells itself. The sly smile in the music communicates the notion that the singer is getting away with the best prank imaginable while the whole world watches, with the whole world asking, "Who was that masked man?" when the record ends, the world then playing the record again and again as if by doing so the world could find out. The man before you is young and beautiful, charming, urbane, utterly cool, yet at any moment a sense of weightlessness, of pure fun, can break out and engulf the entirety of his performance. The man is a trickster. For "White Christmas," the other Drifters begin respectfully. They finish a verse—and then the

Imp of the Perverse arrives, McPhatter singing like Rumpel-stiltskin promising to spin straw into gold, leaving the nation dumbfounded with his whirling falsetto, open-mouthed in the face of a reversal of the country's shared cultural symbolism that in pop music would not be matched until Jimi Hendrix used "The Star-Spangled Banner" to speak to the Founding Fathers.

"Money Honey" is a comic song, but in McPhatter's performance the humor is all in the bottled-up urgency he gives Jesse Stone's lyrics, and the humor is real life. "Without love there is nothing," McPhatter would sing softly in one of his solo hits; the message of "Money Honey" is that without money there's no love. Still, there's the thrill of the chase. Part of the delight of "Money Honey" is waiting to hear if the next verse can top the one before it, tell a better story, and from the landlord at the door to the realization that the singer needs a new girlfriend—and the girlfriend a new boyfriend—it always does. But the overriding shock is that as all parts of the music come together, you are present at a creation—the creation or the discovery of rock 'n' roll. The special energy that only comes when people sense they are putting something new into the world, something that will leave the world not quite as it was, rises up. "Ah-*ooooom*," begin tenors Bill Pinkney and Andrew Thrasher, bass Willie Ferbie, and baritone Gerhart Thrasher, low and ominous, and then McPhatter begins the quest that will occupy him for the rest of the song: the quest for his rent. He takes the first verse full of enthusiasm; there's a stumble on the drums as there will be on every verse, but he leaps over it. The second verse is congenial—he's trying to get his dearly beloved to open her purse—but on the third verse it's her words that are coming out of his mouth: *We're through.* McPhatter bears down, almost scared, and everything in the music tightens, goes hard and mean. McPhatter shouts for the instrumental break, saxophonist Sam "The Man" Taylor comes in for his solo— and he burns it, rocketing the music out of anything it's prepared you for, the beat now rushing upstream too fast to track, and then McPhatter screams.

There is nothing like this scream—not in McPhatter's own music, or in any of the music to follow his, as Elvis Presley and Jackie Wilson and Sam Cooke tried to wrap their voices around their memories of McPhatter's, as something of his drive and flair filtered down over the years to the countless singers who wouldn't recognize his name. It's a scream of surprise—it's the scream of a man watching a door blow out, a man who's made it to the other side and is ready now to reach back and pull everyone over. The record ends conventionally, and you wonder: did that happen?

As if from the other side of the earth, you can hear something similar in Robert Johnson. Though the recordings Son House made in 1930 can seem like the summation of all the knowledge amassed by the divines of the School of the Mississippi Delta Blues, in comparison with the recordings Johnson made in 1936 and 1937, when he was in his mid-twenties—"Come on in My Kitchen," "Traveling Riverside Blues," "Hellhound on My Trail"—most of the masters who preceded him sing and play as men who have accepted the world as they found it. They speak the language of what is known; playing and singing with more force and more delicacy, with lines that are like staircases to ceilings and windows opening onto walls—ceilings and walls that the music opens as if they were doors, and which in the same way the music then closes behind itself—Johnson speaks the language of what isn't. That isn't why most of those who came before him lived on long after Johnson's murder at a Mississippi juke joint in 1938; it does make his music a kind of witness to his death. Inside the figures he made on the guitar and the shadings of his voice there are always possibilities other than those that are stated. At the highest pitch of his music each note that is played implies another that isn't; each emotion that is expressed hints at what can't be said. For all of its elegance and craft the music is unstable at its core—each song is at once an attempt to escape from the world as everyone around the singer believes it to be, and a dream that that world is not a prison but a homecoming. Like the Drifters or Dion and the Belmonts, Johnson is momentarily in the air, flying just as one does in a dream, looking down in wonder at where you are, then soaring as if it's the most natural thing in the world.

Before "Like a Rolling Stone," Johnson and the Drifters may have come closer to the total sound than anyone else. The desire could be defined even if its realization was impossible—maybe it could be defined because its realization was impossible. The total sound would be all-encompassing, all-consuming. For as long as it lasted that sound would be the world itself—and who knew what would happen when you left that world and returned to the world that, before you heard the sound, seemed complete and finished?

"Like a Rolling Stone" stays in the air. That's its challenge to itself: to stay up for six full minutes, never looking down. When the song ends it disappears into the air, leaving the earth to all the men and women scurrying through the tunnels and traps of the rest of the country mapped on *Highway 61 Revisited*, the set of songs it would begin.

As Al Kooper has always told the story, he was just supposed to watch. On June 16, the day after the first, abortive stabs at the song, for which he wasn't present, he showed up at Columbia's Studio A as a guest of the producer, Tom Wilson. Born in 1931, dead of a heart attack in 1978, Wilson was a Harvard graduate in economics; in the late 1950s and early 1960s he produced records by John Coltrane and Cecil Taylor. In 1965 he was one of the few black producers at a major label, but after the sessions for "Like a Rolling Stone" he was replaced as Dylan's producer and cut out of producing Simon and Garfunkel, who would prove to be a far more lucrative act. He went on to MGM/Verve, where he put his name on *Freak Out*, by Frank Zappa's Mothers of Invention, their 1967

Playback: from left to right, Roy Halee, Pete Duryea (at rear), Tom Wilson, Albert Grossman, Bob Dylan, Vinnie Fusco (at rear), Sandy Speiser (foreground), Danny Kalb

"America Drinks and Goes Home" marathon *Absolutely Free*, and the Velvet Underground's 1968 *White Light/White Heat*, which at its most relentless sounded as if it had been recorded in a cardboard box. Wilson had an open mind and open ears. He was a formidable character, but he wasn't there when Kooper arrived, and Kooper, at twenty-one a longtime veteran of the music business—teenage guitarist for the Royal Teens (after their one hit, "Short Shorts," number 3 in 1958), songwriter, song-hustler, recording artist ("Sick Manny's Gym" with Leo De Lyon and the Musclemen in 1960, "Parchman Farm" under his own name in 1963), New York session guitarist—had no intention of kibitzing in the control booth. He sat down with the other musicians Wilson had called for the session, most of them people he already knew: drummer Bobby Gregg, organist Paul Griffin, bassist Joe Macho, Jr., and Bruce Langhorne, guitarist on "Bob Dylan's 115th Dream," but this day holding his treasured giant Turkish tambourine. Then Dylan arrived with Michael Bloomfield.

I was playing in a club in Chicago, I guess it was about 1956, or nineteen-*sixty*. And I was sittin' there, I was sittin' in a restaurant, I think it was, probably across the street, or maybe it was even part of the club, I'm not sure—but a guy came down and said that he played guitar. So he had his guitar with him, and he begin to play, I said, "Well, what *can* you play?" and he played all kinds of things, I don't know if you've ever heard of a man, does Big Bill *Broonzy* ring a bell? Or, ah, Sonny Boy Williamson, that type of thing? He just played circles, around anything I could play, and I always remembered that.

Anyway, we were back in New York, think it was about 1963 or 1964, and I needed a guitar player on a session I was doin', and I called up—I didn't, I even remembered his name—and he came in and recorded an album at that time; he was working in the Paul Butterfield *Blues* Band. He played with me on the record, and I think we played some other dates. I haven't seen him *too much* since then. He played on "Like a *Rollin'* Stone." And he's here tonight, give him a hand, Michael Bloomfield!

—Bob Dylan, introducing Michael Bloomfield as a guest guitarist on "Like a Rolling Stone," Warfield Theatre, San Francisco, 15 November 1980

Bloomfield was born in Chicago in 1943; as a barely teenage guitarist he grew up on the radio and in dance bands. He tried to play like Scotty Moore played with Elvis, and mastered Chuck Berry; he followed Cliff Gallup, guitarist for Gene Vincent, and James Burton, whose attack on Dale Hawkins's 1957 "Susie-Q"—like a mugging—made the record a password. He moved through folk music and country blues, and then into the blues world of his own city. He ran a blues club; when he was eighteen he played piano in a band behind blues singer Big Joe Williams, and then he played with everybody else. "You had to be as good as Otis Rush, you had to be as good as Buddy Guy, as good as Freddie King, whatever instrument you played at the time, you had to be as good as they were," he once said. "And who wanted to be bad on the South Side? Man, you were exposed all over. Right in that city where you lived, in one night you could hear Muddy Waters, Howlin' Wolf . . . Big Walter, Little Walter, Junior Wells, Lloyd Jones, just dozens of different blues singers, some famous, some not so famous. They were all part of the blues, and you could work with them if you were good enough." He found his own sound: "I play sweet blues," he said in 1968. "I can't explain it. I want to be singing. I want to be sweet." "If I could be anything in the world," a friend said that year, "it would be to be Mike Bloomfield's notes."

But as Bloomfield found his sound he couldn't keep it. In 1967 he left Paul Butterfield, as he had left Dylan after a single show, at the Newport Folk Festival in 1965, and formed the enormously publicized Electric Flag, which debuted at the Monterey Pop Festival in 1967, where the band's confused blues pastiches and soul tributes were upstaged by Jimi Hendrix, who after singing "Like a Rolling Stone" lit his guitar on fire and prayed to it, the Who, who before smashing their instruments swirled the crowd with eight minutes of their little operetta "A Quick One While He's Away" ("You're forgiven!" Pete Townshend shouted at the audience of music business insiders), and, especially, Big Brother and the Holding Company's version of Willie Mae Thornton's "Ball and Chain," the performance that made Janis Joplin an international star. Bloomfield's band broke up after a single album. He made

"Supersession" LPs with Al Kooper and Stephen Stills, late of Buffalo Springfield, all of them trading on glories just past ("Lousy show," a story from the time had someone saying to one of the three. "Yeah, but we got a couple of albums out of it," was supposedly the reply); he made solo records, played again with Butterfield and Muddy Waters, but fewer were listening with each release, and there was less and less reason to. He sank into heroin and alcoholism, and pulled himself out. He taught guitar classes; he did soundtrack work for Mitchell Brothers porn movies. In 1981 he was found in his car, dead of an overdose, near his house in San Francisco; he was thirty-seven. Without his presence in "Like a Rolling Stone" his name might be forgotten today. Because of it he is still on the air.

I first met Bob at a Chicago club called "The Bear," where he was performing. I went down there because I had read the liner notes on one of his albums that described him as a "hot-shot folk guitar player, bluesy, blah-blah-whee, Merle Travis picking, this and that." The music on his album was really lame, I thought. He couldn't sing, he couldn't play.

I went down to the Bear to cut him with my guitar. I wanted to show him how to play music, and when I got there I couldn't believe it. His personality. He was so nice. I went there with my wife and we just talked. He was the coolest, nicest cat. We talked about Sleepy John Estes and Elvis' first records and rock and roll ... He was a nervous, crazy guy.

When Dylan called, Bloomfield said, "I bought a Fender, a really good guitar for the first time in my life, without a case. A Telecaster."

I went to his house first to hear the tunes. The first thing I heard was "Like a Rolling Stone." He wanted me to get the concept of it, how to play it. I figured he wanted blues, string bending, because that's what I do. He said, "Hey, man, I don't want any of that B. B. King stuff." So, OK, I really fell apart. What the heck does he want? We messed around with the song. I played the way that he dug and he said it was groovy.

Then we went to the session. Bob told me, "You talk to the musicians, man, I don't want to tell them anything." So we get to the session. I didn't know anything about it. All these studio cats are standing around. I come in like a dumb punk with my guitar over my back, no case, and I'm telling people about this and that, and this is the arrangement, and do this on the bridge. These are like the heaviest studio musicians in New York. They looked at me like I was crazy.

—Michael Bloomfield, "Impressions of Bob Dylan," *Hit Parader*, June 1968

Tom Wilson was still missing. "It was already inappropriate that I had gone and sat there with a guitar," Kooper says. "And then Bloomfield cured me of that. Tom Wilson never saw me out there with a guitar. That was a very lucky part of the day—not being caught by Tom Wilson, and not being stuck having to play guitar next to Mike Bloomfield. He was way over my head. I never heard a white person play like that in my life. Until that moment."

Wilson returned; Kooper was already back in the control room, out of the game. The players worked toward a sound, but it was off; Wilson moved Paul Griffin from the Hammond organ to the piano, looking for a brighter feeling. "I walked over to Tom Wilson and said, 'Hey, I got a really good part for this on the organ,'" Kooper says. "He just sort of scoffed at me: 'Ah, man, you're not an organ player. You're a guitar player.' Then he got called to the phone. And my reasoning said, 'He didn't say *no*'—so I went out there." "It was a terror tactic," Kooper says. "There's a moment, it's actually recorded, where [Wilson] says, 'OK, this is take number whateveritis,' and he goes, '*Heyyyy*—what're *you* doin' out there?' I just start laughing—and he goes, 'Awright, awright, here we go, this is take something, "Like a Rolling Stone."'" So there was that moment when he could have yanked me out of there. I thanked God that he didn't. It would have been so embarrassing." So the ensemble was set.

The song they were about to record was not a natural song. As a set of words to sing it was what Dylan always said it was, something pulled out of something else, a story made out of an impulse: "Telling someone something they didn't know, telling them they were lucky." One line didn't necessarily pull the next one after it; sometimes a phrase fell back on the one coming up behind it. Compared only to the songs that on *Highway 61 Revisited* would sail in its wake, "Like a Rolling Stone" lacks the balance of the title song, with lines and images whipping back at each other at full speed:

> Now the fifth daughter on the twelfth night
> Told the first father that things weren't right

It doesn't approach the visionary momentum of "Desolation Row," where a whole new world is built out of the debris of the old and every character in the song, from Einstein to T. S. Eliot, the Blind Commissioner to Cinderella, seems capable of changing into every other. As words on paper, it falls short of "Ballad of a Thin Man" in vehemence. There is nothing careful about the language. Dylan usually had the instincts, or the studied judgment, to avoid the momentary slang and contrived neologisms that would date his songs, box them up and turn them into artifacts. Perhaps because of his scholar's sense of how folk ballads and early blues came together in the fifty years after the Civil War—sharing countless author-less phrases so alive to their objects ("forty dollars won't pay my fine," anybody could say that, and everybody did) that even when the phrases passed out of common usage they could communicate as poetry ("drink up your blood like wine," not too many could get away with that, and not too many tried)—Dylan had a feel for making phrases of his own that no matter how unlikely

I got forty red white and blue shoestrings
And a thousand telephones that don't ring

could seem not made but found. His sense of time, or time-lessness, only rarely failed him; usually the momentum in his music passed over moments of laziness, when it was easier to plug in words of the day than to find the words that were right. "Just about blew my mind" flies by without damage in "Bob Dylan's 115th Dream," and "Blows the mind most bit-terly" is carried off by the rhythm in "It's Alright, Ma (I'm Only Bleeding)." But street talk can change by the week, and by 1965, "Where it's at" had lost the charge of real speech it carried in Sam Cooke's "That's Where It's At" just a year before. The words stuck out in "Like a Rolling Stone," with the expression now less a phrase than a catchphrase, less words you used to say something than an advertising slogan you repeated in spite of yourself. It sounds cheap, broken, as if the writer was in too much of a hurry to get it right, or didn't care, and the song trips over it, momentarily goes blank as the words are sung. And then the next line is sung.

Something big is about to happen. At the heart of the song, the prince who after years of wandering the land as a vagabond is ready to tell what he has learned; at a fair he gathers twos and threes to hear his promise that he is about to reveal the secret of the kingdom, and soon there is a crowd.

In the studio in New York City, the fanfare opens, with small notes on the piano dancing like fairies over the low, steady pulse from an organ you hear but don't register. There is a false sense that you can still wait for whatever it is that is about to happen to happen. But when you emerge from the reverie of the song as it begins—in that rising sun of a fanfare there is an invitation to look over your shoulder at a receding, familiar landscape, as if the story that is about to begin is a story you have heard a thousand times ("It's such an old story," Bloomfield said)—the train has already left the station. "Once upon a time," and you are not the child falling asleep as someone reads from Grimm's Fairy Tales, the violence and gore removed, the illustrations glowing with blonde hair and blue eyes. You're in the story, about to be cooked, eaten, dismembered, left behind, and as in an early Disney animation the trees in the forest are reaching out their branches like hands and tearing at your clothes. That is what the singer is saying as the music blows all around you, but this isn't a nightmare, and if it were you wouldn't want to wake up. This is a great adventure. As if keeping a secret from yourself—the secret of how bad the story sounds and how good it feels—you cover your eyes with your hands and peek through your fingers at the screen.

Bombs are going off everywhere, and every bomb is a word. "*DIDN'T*"—"*STEAL*"—"*USED*"—"*INVISIBLE*": they are part of the story, but in the way they are sung—declaimed, hammered, thrown down from the mountain to shatter among the crowd at the foot—each word is also the story itself. You are drawn into single words as if they are caves within the song. Why one word is bigger than another—or more threatening, or more seductive—makes no obvious narrative sense. The words aren't merely bombs, they're land mines. They have been planted in the song for you to find, which is to say planted that they might find you. Each word lies flat on a stone in the field, spelled out, "YOU," "ALRIGHT," "ALIBIS," "KICKS," "THAT," "BE," "NEVER," but there is no way at all to know which one will blow up when you step on it.

Like a waterway opening, the organ comes in to stake its claim on the song halfway through the first verse, just after Dylan finishes setting up the story and begins to bear down hard; just before *"You used to/ Laugh about—"* The song is under way, the ship is already pitching, and the high, keening sound Kooper is making, pressing down on a chord as it streams into the song, is something to hold onto. This side of the story is just beginning, a step behind the story you are already being told; this sound within the sound tells you the story can't end soon, and that it won't be rushed. The sound the organ traces is determined, immune, almost part of another song. "I couldn't hear the organ, because the speaker was on the other side of the room covered with blankets," Kooper says, speaking as someone caught up in the uncertainty, the blind leading the blind over a cliff. "I'm used to there being a music director. Having grown up in the studio, there was always someone in charge, whether it was the arranger, the artist, or the producer. There was no one in charge at that session—in charge of the general chaos. I didn't completely know the song yet. I do have big ears—that was my biggest advantage. In the verses, I waited an eighth note before I hit the chord. The band would play the chord and I would play after that." But as the song goes on, the organ becomes the conductor of its own drama. For the song it is the shaping hand.

Bloomfield has entered the verse rolling a golden wheel. There is a great glow in the circular patterns he is tracing, but even as the glow warms the listener it is fading into a kind of undertow, now pulling against anything in the music that is still prophesying an open road. Now there is a deep, implacable hum coming from Bloomfield's guitar, a sound seemingly independent of the musician himself, a loose wire or a frayed connection playing its own version of the song.

No sound holds in the cataclysm the song is becoming; its general chaos is its portrait of everyday life. There is nothing remarkable in the words Dylan is singing so far, no oddly named characters, just someone who once tossed money at people who had none and is now wondering how far she's willing to go to get some of her own. But as the first verse tilts toward its last line Bloomfield is shooting out of the verse, playing louder than before, hurry and triumph in his fingers. You can feel the song turning, but there is no sense yet of what's around the turn.

What is around the turn is a clearing, where the musicians charging around the bend find themselves in Enfield, Connecticut, in 1741, with the singer already there to meet them for the chorus—the singer in the form of Jonathan Edwards pronouncing his sermon "Sinners in the Hands of an Angry God" to parishioners who are tearing at their hair and begging him to stop, and the musicians are immediately alive to the drama. "I tried to stay out of Bloomfield's way," Kooper says, "because he was playing great stuff. *'Your next meeeeeal'*— on the five chord just before the chorus, where he does that 'diddle-oo da diddle-oo,' that was a great lick. I didn't want to step on that. And then he would play that coming out of the chorus, too. The other places, I had room to play, because Michael was not playing lead in those places: in the chorus." Kooper is still following his own road, but now it comes into full relief; each single line he offers is so clear, moving forward so deliberately, that you can see the track his notes are cutting. The singer is raging and thundering in the air above, paying no mind to anything anyone else has to say but his body absorbing it all, and everything his body absorbs goes into his voice, which grows bigger with every word. Bloomfield's golden wheel, now bigger than before and even brighter, and more dangerous, a wheel that as its light blinds you will roll right over you, carries the singer out of the clearing and into the next verse. In a minute and a half, a verse and a chorus, more has already happened than in any other song the year has produced.

The feeling in the music in the second verse is more triumphant. Bloomfield's lines are longer, more like a hawk in the sky than deer leaping a ravine. The rest follow a steady march, and the story seems headed to a conclusion; near the end of the verse is perhaps the most astonishing moment of all, when, out of instinct, out of desire, out of a smile somewhere in his memory, Bloomfield finds the sound of a great *whoosh*, and for an instant a rising wind blows right through the rest of the music as if the song is a shotgun shack. Is that what allows the singer to whirl in the air, striking out in all directions? There's a desperation, something close to fear, in the way Dylan throws out *"used to it"*—the words seem to pull the person in the song off her feet, leaving her in the gutter, stunned, filth running over her, the singer's reach to pull her out falling short, but there's no time to go back: the chorus has arrived again. With its first line, those four simple words, how does it feel, an innocuous question, really, you feel that this time the singer is demanding more from the words, more from the person to whom they are addressed. In the verses he has chased her, harried her, but the arrival of the chorus vaults him in front of her; as she flees him he appears before her, pointing, shouting—and the person to whom all this is addressed is no longer merely the girl named by the song. That person is now at once that girl and whoever is listening. The song has put the listener on the spot.

You are listening to the song on the radio, in 1965 or forty years later. "Like a Rolling Stone" is not on the radio forty years after its release as often as it was in the second half of 1965—but you might be able to count on hearing it more frequently in 2005 than you did in 1966, when it was last year's hit. On the radio, where the tambourine is inaudible, the piano seems like an echo of the guitar, and the organ could be playing to the drums, you can hear Dylan's up-and-down rhythm guitar and Joe Macho's bass as a single instrument. Dylan and Macho have heard each other, and they have locked into a single pattern, the bass supporting the guitar, the guitar extending the bass. This is the spine of the song, you realize, or its heartbeat, banging against the spine. It's the simplest thing in the world: "very punky," as Kooper hears it. "Ragged and filthy." But the song must be almost over—the second verse has passed, and the chorus has nearly run out its string. The song has already demanded more from you than anything else you've ever heard. You want more, but that's what a fade at the end of a record is for, isn't it, the sound disappearing into silence, to leave you wanting more?

Even now, when it is no shock that there is more, as there was when the record first appeared on the radio in 1965, no surprise that the disc jockey is actually going to turn the record over to see what happens, to play the whole thing, as in the first week or so of the song's release many disc jockeys did not, it is still a shock. The arrival of the third verse, the announcement that the story is not over, is like Roosevelt announcing for a third term.

"Like a Rolling Stone" wasn't the first six-minute Top 40 hit, or the first to be cut in half and pressed onto two sides of a 45. In 1959 both Ray Charles's "What'd I Say," which was longer than six minutes, and the Isley Brothers' "Shout," which was shorter, but more dramatically flipped from side A to side B ("Now, *waaaaiiiiit* a minute," cried the leader as the first side reached the out groove), were hits, and "What'd I Say" was enormous, inescapable. But these were dance records, not story-telling records. They swept the listener up and carried the listener along, but they did not implicate the listener; they did not suggest that the song had anything to do with the moral failings of the people listening, or that its story was their story, whether they liked it or not. All "Like a Rolling Stone" shared with "What'd I Say" and "Shout" was their length and their delirium.

In *Don't Look Back*, in England in the spring of 1965, the film teases the viewer with the notion that you can see "Like a Rolling Stone" first take shape in the film itself. Dylan and Baez and Dylan's sidekick Bob Neuwirth are in a hotel room; Dylan is singing Hank Williams's "Lost Highway," from 1949. It was a rare Williams song that he didn't write. "Once he was in California hitchhiking to Alba, Texas, to visit his sick mother," Myrtie Payne, the widow of Leon Payne, the song's composer, told the country music historian Dorothy Horstman. "He was unable to get a ride and finally got help from the Salvation Army. It was while he was waiting for help that he wrote this song." With Baez singing harmony, it's the first time in the film that Dylan seems engaged by a song. "I was just a lad, nearly twenty-two," he sings, as if the words are his, with a Hank Williams whine that somehow doesn't seem fake. "Neither good nor bad, just a kid like you." "No, no," says Neuwirth. "There's another verse, 'I'm a rolling *stone.*'" Dylan picks it up, and it's odd that he left it out, because it is the first verse: "I'm a rolling stone, all alone and lost/ For a life of sin, I have paid the cost..." But the words "rolling stone" are swallowed up in the tune—"stone" almost fades away as it is sung, wearing down to a pebble as it rolls—and all the words speak for is someone with no will, no desire. Yes, it's a song of freedom: freedom from family, authority, government, work, religion, but most of all from yourself. It's a wastrel's song; not "rolling stone" but "lost highway" is the ruling image, promising that the singer's grave will likely be a ditch on the side of the road.

In "Like a Rolling Stone" you can't hear "Lost Highway" any more readily than you can hear Muddy Waters's 1950 "Rollin' Stone." Cut in Chicago, with Waters playing a big-city electric guitar, the piece was pure Mississippi in its tone, its menace, affirming a tension coiled so tightly in the music that when in a brief guitar solo Waters turns over a single, vibrating note, it seems to bite itself. "Gonna be a rollin' stone/ Sho' nuff be the rollin' stone," the pregnant woman in the first verse chants to herself of the child she's carrying, snapping off the last word again and again with the feeling of a knife quivering in a wall—unless it's the child inside her banging on the door, whispering he'll kill her if she doesn't let him out. Here the rollin' stone gets up and walks like a man, and that's what you hear in Waters's guitar solo, more even than in the way he slides his voice over the words. You hear someone free from values and limits, never mind mothers, fathers, jobs, church, or the county courthouse. He never raises his voice. You get the idea that if he did—

In folk terms it's fables like "Lost Highway" and "Rollin' Stone" that Dylan's image comes from, but if the image of the rolling stone is what seals his song's own fable, that image is not what drives the song. As a song, a performance, a threat, or a gesture, "Like a Rolling Stone" is closer to Dylan's own "A Hard Rain's A-Gonna Fall," from 1963, Elvis Presley's 1961 "Can't Help Falling in Love," the Animals' 1964 "House of the Rising Sun," Sonny Boy Williamson's "Don't Start Me Talkin'" and Elvis's "Mystery Train," both from 1955, the Stanley Brothers' 1947 "Little Maggie," or Noah Lewis's 1930 "New Minglewood Blues." ("I was born in the desert, raised up in the lion's den," Lewis sang coolly, as if he were presenting himself as the new sheriff in town. "My number one occupation, is stealing womens from their men.")* "Like a Rolling

---

* Sometimes it's in Dylan's own performances of these songs that you can hear "Like a Rolling Stone," though not always: his desultory 1970 recording of "Can't Help Falling in Love," omitted from the already thrown-together *Self Portrait* and included on the bottom-of-the-barrel release *Dylan* in 1973 (Dylan had temporarily jumped to another label and Columbia was attempting to embarrass him by releasing the worst stuff they could find), said nothing about anything. His 1992 "Little Maggie" was stark, syncopated, and deathly, but it owed nothing to the Stanley Brothers; if Dylan drew on their performance for "Like a Rolling Stone," it was for its structure, its melody, and most of all its

Stone" is closer to Will Bennett's irresistibly distracted 1929
"Railroad Bill," which is fifteen combinations of two-line
verses and a one-line refrain in under three minutes, including sets about weaponry ("Buy me a gun, just as long as my
arm/ Kill everybody, ever done me wrong"), throwing everything away and heading west, drinking, domesticity, and the
outlaw Railroad Bill himself, who never worked and never
will. In its headlong drive into the street, its insistence on
saying everything because tomorrow it will be too late—to
speak as a prophet, someone who, burdened with knowledge
he didn't want but, having received it, is forced to pass on—
"Like a Rolling Stone" probably owes more to Allen Ginsberg's 1955 "Howl" than to any song.

If any or all of these things is a source of "Like a Rolling
Stone," or an inspiration, like "Lost Highway" or "Rollin' Stone"
they say little about why the song is what it is. If there is a

---

[*continued*] lift, a sense of triumph. The Animals' "House of the Rising Sun," at
four and a half minutes in its full-length version, was taken from the broken
reading Dylan gave the song on *Bob Dylan* two years before; with the kind of
reach beyond a song's past or even its future that would power "Like a Rolling
Stone," a five-man British blues band from Newcastle transformed an American folk ballad about a New Orleans whorehouse into an international hit that
more than forty years later still circles the globe. But when Dylan sang "Don't
Start Me Talkin'" on *The Late Show with David Letterman* in 1984 he was plainly
possessed by the song, by the chance it gave him to run over everyone in
town ("I'll tell EVERYTHING I know!" he shouted with superhuman glee);
when he threw "New Minglewood Blues" off his stages in the 1990s, his band
crashing down on "born" and "den" as he ripped the words away from them,
every line built on the last until you couldn't see the top of their staircase.

model for "Like a Rolling Stone," it may be in the long, dramatic story-songs made by Mississippi blues players Son House and Garfield Akers—music that, as collected in 1962 on *Really! The Country Blues*, an obscure, hard-to-find album on the fanatical country blues label Origin Jazz Library, Dylan knew well.

On House's 1930 "My Black Mama," more than six minutes and twenty seconds on both sides of a Paramount 78, and Akers's 1929 "Cottonfield Blues," exactly six minutes on the two sides of his Vocalion ten-inch, the songs begin almost identically. "Oh, hey, black mama, what's the matter with you?" says House. "I said, looky here, mama, well just what are you trying to do?" says Akers. Both songs end almost mystically. In "My Black Mama," the woman who was trouble in Part 1 is dead in Part 2. The singer is summoned: "I looked down in her face," he says; you can feel her face already rotting. When he sings, in his last verse, his deep voice seemingly deepening with every syllable, "I fold my arms and I walked away," you can feel him walk off the earth. In "Cottonfield Blues" the woman who was trouble in Part 1 is gone in Part 2; as Akers sings commonplace lines in his high, thin voice, he makes you feel that they have never been sung before. He stretches his words across their vowels so naturally, so inevitably, somehow, that you picture the singer on a mountaintop, singing across a valley, making his own echo, but when the song hits home

I'm gonna write you a letter, I'm gonna mail it in the air
I'm gonna write you a letter, I'm gonna mail it in the air

Says I know you will catch it, babe, in this world somewhere
Says I know you'll catch it, mama, in the world somewhere

you see that Akers is the letter and that he is in the air, traveling somewhere out of reach of the U.S. Mail.

"My Black Mama" is slow, all of its drama bottled up; as it
moves forward the pressure is never released. Akers jumps
"Cottonfield Blues" on his guitar, his technique so primitive
that for all he has to tell you about Mississippi in 1929 he
could be playing in Manchester in 1977 on the Buzzcocks'
"Boredom," their punk theses-nailed-to-the-nightclub-door.
Akers pushes his story so fast you can feel he's afraid of it, and
House makes no effort to hide the fact that he is afraid of his.
Each is such an old story—and each is utterly singular. Each
man says the same thing: to tell a story, you must take as
much time as you need. The length of "My Black Mama" and
"Cottonfield Blues" is the axis of their art; when you reach the
end of either, you have been taken all the way through a crisis
in a certain person's life. Because the artist, speaking in the
first person, has shaped that crisis so that his response to it
becomes an argument about a whole way of being in the
world, you have not only been through a crisis. Taken to its
essence, the artist has described his life as such, guided you
through the strange and foreign country of his birth, educa-
tion, deeds, and failures, right up to the point of death.

With "Like a Rolling Stone" too, its six minutes—six minutes to break the limits of what could go on the radio, of

what kind of story the radio could tell; at first the label on the 45 read 5.59, as if that would be less intimidating—is the beginning and the end of what the record is about and what it is for. When the record is over, when it disappears into the clamor of its own fade to silence, or the next commercial, you feel as if you have been on a journey, as if you have traversed the whole of a country that is neither strange nor foreign, because it is self-evidently your own—even if, in the first three minutes, the journey only went as far as your own city limits. The pace is about to pick up.

When "Like a Rolling Stone" smashes into its third verse everything is changed. The mystery tramp who appeared out of nowhere at the end of the second verse has left his cousins all over this one. Everyone has a strange name, everyone is a riddle, there's nobody you recognize, but everybody seems to know who you are. "Ah, you—" Dylan shouts, riding over the hump of the second chorus and into the third verse; the increase in vehemence caused by something so tiny as the adding of a syllable of frustration to the already accusing "you" is proof of how much pressure has built up. The sound Bloomfield makes is like Daisy's voice—"the sound of money"—and like Gatsby Bloomfield is reaching for it, but as soon as it is in the air he steps back from it, counting off the beat as if he is just James Gatz, counting his pennies. He is banging the gong of the rhythm as if he is hypnotized by it, each glorious note bending back toward the one before it. As the band seems to play more slowly, as if recognizing the

story in the song for the first time—a congress of delegates
drawn from all over the land, all speaking at once and all giving a version of the same speech—the singer moves faster, as
if he knows what's coming and has to stop it. He reaches the
last line of the verse, holds the last word as long as he can
hold his breath, and then as the song tips into the third chorus everything shatters.

The intensity of the first words out of Dylan's mouth
make it seem as if a pause has preceded them, as if he has
gathered up every bit of energy in his being and concen-
trated it on a single spot, and as if you can hear him draw
that breath. "How does it feel" doesn't come out of his
mouth; each word explodes in it. And here you understand
what Dylan meant when he said, in 1966, speaking of the
pages of noise he'd scribbled, "I had never thought of it as a
song, until one day I was at the piano, and on the paper it
was singing, 'How does it feel?'" Dylan may sing the verses;
the chorus sings him.

With this moment every element in the song doubles in
size. It doubles in weight. There is twice as much song as
there was before. An avenger the first time "How does it feel"
takes him over here, the second time the line sounds Dylan is
despairing, bereft and sorrowful, but by now, moments after
he himself has blown the song to pieces, the song has gotten
away from him. Kooper's simple, straight, elegant lines are
breaking up, shooting out in all directions, as if Dylan's first
"How does it feel" was the song's Big Bang and Kooper is

determined to catch every fragment of the song as it flies away. As the chorus begins to climb a mountain that wasn't in the chorus before, Kooper finds himself in the year before, in the middle of Alan Price's organ solo in the Animals' "House of the Rising Sun," a record that to this day has lost none of its grime and none of its grandeur. Price's solo was frenzied, its tones thick and dark; it was a deep dive into a whirlpool Price himself had made, and Kooper is playing from inside the vortex, each line rushing up and out, nailing the flag of the song to its mast.

Nothing could follow this. In the fourth verse, everyone's timing is gone. The "Ah" that swung the first line of the third verse is here a long "Ahhhhhh" that flattens its own first line. Bobby Gregg, whose drum patterns in the first verse had given the song shape before the musicians found the shape within the song, fumbles as if he has accidentally kicked over his kit. Everyone is fighting to get the song back—and it's the words that rescue it, that for the first time take the song away from its sound. The words are slogans, but they are arresting, and if "When you ain't got nothing, you got nothing to lose" sounds like something you might read on a Greenwich Village sampler, a bohemian version of "Home Sweet Home," "You're invisible now, you got no secrets to conceal" is not obvious, it is confusing.

Confused—and justified, exultant, free from history with a world to win—is exactly where the song means to leave you. There is a last chorus, like the last verse spinning off its

With Michael Bloomfield

axis, and then Dylan's dive for his harmonica, and then a crazy-quilt of high notes that light out for the territory the song itself has opened up.

Fifteen years later, when Dylan invited Bloomfield onto the stage at the Warfield Theatre to play the song again, Dylan was filled with Jesus, and Bloomfield was just a Jew, washed-up, a junkie whose words were as empty as his eyes, a pariah. Bob Johnston, the producer who would replace Tom Wilson after "Like a Rolling Stone," was there for the show. Bloomfield approached him. "Can you help me?" he said. "No one will talk to me." Bloomfield promised he was off drugs, that he wasn't drinking, that he had gotten his life back, but Johnston had already heard him play. After each phrase from Dylan, Bloomfield fingered his rolling notes, but he couldn't play the song. In the way that he could only play the record—in the way that he couldn't hear the music, couldn't respond to the other musicians, or to Dylan, or to the three-woman gospel chorus, in the way that, like so many Dylan guitarists who over the years, in city after city, have copied Bloomfield's notes as blankly as Bloomfield was doing this night, he could only copy himself—he was lost, and then he was incoherent, a ruin. But as he so rarely would after the first year he toured with "Like a Rolling Stone," this night Dylan is flying with the song, energized by the story. As it goes on he hits everything harder:

He's not *selling any al-i-bis*

As you stare into the vacuum of his eyes

And say, do you want to, ha ha, make a *deeeeaaaallll*

He opens the second chorus as if he is unfurling the flag
that Tashtego, or Al Kooper, nailed to the sinking mast of the
Pequod at the end of *Moby-Dick,* and as it did in 1965, fresh
wind blows through the music. It almost seems as if Dylan is
defending the song from Bloomfield—trying to rescue the
song Bloomfield must have still carried somewhere inside
himself from the broken man who could no longer really play
it; defending the song or, from his own side, trying to give it
back. "In them you can hear a young man, with an amazing
amount of young man's energy, the kind of thing you would
find in the early Pete Townshend or the early Elvis," Bloomfield said two days before his death, speaking to the radio
producer Tom Yates, talking about the songs Robert Johnson
cut more than forty years before. "You can hear this in
Robert's records; it just leaps off at you from the turntable."
Was he asking his interviewer to say to him, "Yes, but you
played like that, too"? Could it be that in the unfinished fable
of the record they made together in 1965, Michael Bloomfield played out the fable of self-destruction in "Lost Highway," and Bob Dylan the fable of mastery in "Rollin' Stone"?
"Michael Bloomfield!" Dylan said as the song ended that
night at the Warfield. "Y'all go see him if he's playing around
town."

PART THREE

CHAPTER SEVEN

On the Air

Soon after "Like a Rolling Stone" was recorded Tom Wilson was fired as Bob Dylan's producer; determining why and by whom is not much easier than solving the mystery of who replaced Beatles drummer Pete Best with Ringo Starr. Albert Grossman, Dylan's manager at the time, isn't talking; he died in 1986. Wilson never spoke about it; neither has Clive Davis, the corporate attorney who in June of 1965 became administrative vice-president of Columbia Records and immediately moved to take over everything that wasn't registered, copyrighted, or locked in a safe; he famously became president of the company in 1967, was even more famously fired in 1973 and, through his label Arista and his work with performers from Whitney Houston to Patti Smith, has been an untouchable music-business god ever since. Dylan joined the Know-Nothing Party: "All I know," he has always said, "is that I was out recording one day, and Tom had always been there—I had no reason to think he wasn't going to be there—and I looked up one day and Bob was there."

"I never had a cross word with Dylan," says Bob Johnston, who after taking over the sessions that would result in *Highway 61 Revisited* produced Dylan's 1966 *Blonde on Blonde*, and after that *John Wesley Harding* in 1967, *Nashville Skyline* in 1969, and *Self Portrait* and *New Morning* in 1970—as well as hugely popular generational balm from Simon and Garfunkel (inheriting the version of "The Sounds of Silence" that Wilson had overdubbed with drums and electric instrumentation) and cult noir by the brooding Canadian wise man Leonard Cohen. "I never had a *Fuck you, you do this*. There was never any of that with any artist I ever had, I guess because they knew I *hated* the fucking company and I hated the goddamn *people* at the company—they were fucking all the artists, *always*, out of their money. And—Clive Davis saying, 'Take the drum off "Sounds of Silence."' He said that at a goddamn meeting. Said, 'That drum has got to come off there.' I stood up and said, 'You're right.' And I left the meeting. I went and made a copy, and turned the drum off. And then I made a copy and put *two* drums on it. And I played them the one without the drums, and they all applauded, and said, 'Oh, man, that's just beautiful!' And I released the other one."

Johnston was a canny, ambitious producer with a disarming drawl. He was born in Hillsboro, Texas, in 1932, and grew up in Fort Worth; he started in the music business after service in the Korean War. His grandmother Mamie Jo Adams was a songwriter; his mother, Diane Johnston, composer of "Miles and Miles of Texas," wrote for cowboy and western singers, at the top: Gene Autry, Roy Rogers, and Eddy Arnold. Johnston started out as a writer; after hustling songs in the south and singing with a black trio called the Click Clacks, he moved into the New York song factory at 1650 Broadway, where Al Kooper learned the trade ("That's where I went to church, and college—1650 was where I went to college. I had many classes in that building"), and which housed the storied Aldon Music teams of Carole King and Gerry Goffin, Barry Mann and Cynthia Weil, and Jeff Barry and Ellie Greenwich.* Johnston was at the bottom, churning

---

* "They were doing something in their own right that was just as major as what Dylan was doing," Kooper says of the Aldon writers, whose work for the Drifters ("Up on the Roof"), the Chiffons ("One Fine Day"), the Shirelles ("Will You Love Me Tomorrow"), the Righteous Brothers ("You've Lost that Lovin' Feeling"), and many more of the finest artists of early 1960s rock 'n' roll stands as one of the truest achievements of postwar pop music. Dylan more than anyone ended their careers as songwriters. "You were watching silent movies," Kooper says, speaking of the way Dylan changed what a pop song could be, of how his use of language changed the language of the song. "And all of a sudden there was sound in them. Ohhhh—and that put a lot of people out of work. These handsome people, that talk like this. They were out of work, Jack." They knew it, too: there is no overstating how terrified these great writers were of Bob Dylan. Years before "Like a Rolling Stone," he had all but challenged them to a duel. "Unlike most of the songs nowadays being written uptown in Tin Pan Alley, that's where most of the folk songs come from nowadays," he said on *The Freewheelin' Bob Dylan* in 1963, introducing "Bob Dylan's Blues," "this wasn't written up there—this was written somewhere down in the

out nearly identical follow-ups to whatever someone had hit
with. He recorded himself, for Algonquin, Chic, and Dot
(with his own rocker "I'm Hypnotised"). "Flat Tire" was a
small hit in southern California in 1961, and also Johnston's
last record: a television appearance on the Wink Martindale
show in Los Angeles, where Johnston found himself on the
same bill with Tommy Sands and Ricky Nelson, convinced
him he was too old to be a teenage idol. He moved to
Nashville and went back to writing; in 1964 Elvis Presley
recorded his "It Hurts Me," and after that Johnston wrote
songs for Elvis movies. He became a song-plugger. In
Nashville, that led to producing demos, but Johnston's were

[continued] *United States."* *You're fakes*, heard Goffin and King, nightclub prince
Bobby Darin, star singer Dion, and so many others: *You're fakes, and this is real.* In
2001, for *The Hitmakers*, an A&E documentary on 1650 Broadway, Goffin spoke
in broken, coulda-been-a-contender cadences, sounding beaten down, used
up, passed by: "I wish we had tried more to write some songs that—really
meant something . . . Dylan managed to do something that not one of us was
able to do: put poetry in rock 'n' roll, and just stand up there like a mensch and
sing it. And Carole felt the same way too, and so we had to do something dramatic, so we took all the [demos of] songs that hadn't been placed, not the
songs there had been records on, and smashed them in half. We said, we gotta
grow up, we gotta start writing better songs now." "There was a cultural phenomenon around us that had nothing to do with songwriting," King said on
the same show, sitting around a table with Goffin, Weil, and Mann, a hint of
contempt for the rest of them in her voice. "So it was: *Wait a minute! What's happening, what's going on? Things are changing. How do we write this stuff? How do we fit in?"*
In other words, they were hearing all the questions Dylan was asking in "Like
a Rolling Stone," and beginning to answer them. That they had to devalue
their own work to do it is a testament to how scary the song can be, or how
dangerous.

productions, not sketches: if the song needed it, he'd hire a thirty-voice choir from Fisk University. Columbia brought him to New York in 1964, where he made his name by resurrecting the career of Patti Page. John Hammond, the legendary record man who had written about Robert Johnson for *The New Masses* in 1937 and as a Columbia executive brought Bessie Smith, Billie Holiday, Aretha Franklin, Bob Dylan, and Bruce Springsteen to the label, was Johnston's mentor and protector; in 1965 all Johnston needed as a producer was something he himself actually wanted to hear.

"They were trying to get rid of him," Johnston says of Tom Wilson. "Grossman *hated* him. I have no idea why. He was a nice man. Maybe Grossman didn't like ethnic groups or something—I never thought about it." Bill Gallagher was in charge of production; he told Johnston that Wilson was on his way out. "He called me in and said"—Johnston, a fast talker, drops into a heavy, sententious voice—"'We're going to get rid of Tom.' I said, 'I want Dylan, and Simon.' 'Don't say anything to Tom Wilson,'" Gallagher said. "'Absolutely not,'" Johnston said, as he described the day to Patrick Thomas, a longtime chronicler of his career. "So when I left his office, I went to Wilson and I said, 'Bill Gallagher just called me in and said they're going to get rid of you and that Grossman hates you and they all hate you.' And he said, 'Hell, I knew that anyway.' I said, 'Well, I've got a chance to take over, and I wanted to tell you before I start lobbying.' He said, 'Man, be my guest, because I am out of here any-

way.'" There was lobbying to do; Johnston had Gallagher,
Hammond, and Artists and Repertoire head Bob Mersey ("He
produced and arranged Barbra Streisand, Andy Williams, all
those people") behind him, but neither Dylan nor anyone
around him knew Johnston's name. There was talk of Terry
Melcher, the producer of the Byrds' version of "Mr. Tambourine Man"—number one for Columbia the week after
"Like a Rolling Stone" was cut—and the quintessential Los
Angeles golden boy, at least until 1969, when Charles Manson sent his fiends to kill everyone in Melcher's house,
according to one theory of the Manson case because Melcher
had refused to produce *him*. According to one theory of the
Wilson case, Dylan himself supposedly mentioned Phil Spector, who had dominated the charts for the previous three
years with the most luminous records of the day, from the
Crystals' "He's Sure the Boy I Love" to Darlene Love's "(Today
I Met) The Boy I'm Gonna Marry" to the Ronettes' "Be My
Baby" to "You've Lost that Lovin' Feeling"—which sold eight
million copies.*

---

* "I'd do a Dylan opera with him," Spector said in 1969. "I'd produce him. You
see he's never been produced. He's always gone into the studio on the strength
of his lyrics and they have sold enough records to cover everything up ... He
doesn't really have the time nor do any of his producers necessarily have the
ambition or the talent to really overrule him and debate with him. I would
imagine with Albert Grossman there is a situation of business control just like
it would be with Elvis Presley and Colonel Parker. Maybe nobody has the
guts, balls, or ambition to get in there, but there is no reason unless Dylan
didn't want it. But he could be made to want it."

There was a record made and no one to take responsibility for its release; Johnston stepped into the vacuum and
"Like a Rolling Stone" fell in his lap. One executive
demanded that he rerecord Dylan's vocal: "It's incomprehensible." To Dylan, "Like a Rolling Stone" was a single the
minute he walked out of the studio, if not before he walked
into it. At Columbia, as Johnston remembers it, even as
something that could run from one side of a 45 to the other,
the answer was no: "'*Never put it out.*' They said they would
never put it out. 'Nobody ever had a six-minute single.'"
Johnston knew "What'd I Say," even if Clive Davis or his like
didn't; that, he says, wasn't exactly the point. The point was
the same as it had been with Abel Gance's 1927 *Napoleon*, six
hours long as it played in France, and released in the United
States by MGM with its time cut by more than half, its
screen squeezed, its climactic color triptychs chopped and
bleached, all to ensure that no one in Hollywood would want
to follow suit: "'Nobody ever had a six-minute single'—*and
nobody ever would.*" "We just went ahead and pressed it," Johnston says. "Did the whole fucking thing."*

---

* "John Hammond told me once that I should take over Columbia Records,"
Johnston says, as if telling the story of a broken treaty, of how his Apache
ancestors were driven from their land. "And so I said, 'Well, how do you do it?'
I went up and met with Paley and Stanton [William S. Paley, the legendary
capitalist buccaneer who bought the tiny Columbia Broadcasting System
in 1928, was chairman of the board of CBS; Frank Stanton had been president
of the company since 1946] and those people up there, and they said,
'What would you do if you came into this?' And I says, 'Well, you're not

That has never sounded like the whole story to me. Tom
Wilson's characteristic sound is not at bottom a rock 'n' roll
sound; it's too clean, too discrete. Outside of "Like a Rolling
Stone" there is no feel toward a total sound in the records he
made with Dylan; just the opposite. The instruments stand
out separately. There is no whole sound. There's a harsh
edge—the acrid tone that was everywhere in 1965, the sound
of the time, if not the times.

When the first copies of *Highway 61 Revisited* arrived from
the factory, Tom Wilson's name was missing from "Like a
Rolling Stone," the lead track; Johnston insisted the run be
started over, with Wilson's name restored. But on everything
else on *Highway 61 Revisited*, and even more so on *Blonde on
Blonde*, Johnston's sound is nearly the opposite of Wilson's;
the metal-on-metal screech of "Maggie's Farm" is the farthest
thing from "It Takes a Lot to Laugh, It Takes a Train to Cry"
or "Ballad of a Thin Man." Johnson's sound is not merely

[*continued*] gonna *like* it, and you won't *do* it, but I think the first thing is, you
should get your shit together. And by *that*, you should have the tenth floor, of
attorneys. And the eleventh floor, of accountants. And the *twelfth* floor, of
music. And they should never be allowed, to pass one another. Whatever you
want to do, however you want to cheat, and fuck these artists around, is your
opinion—but at least give them the opportunity of doing something, without
people who tap their foot and whistle out of tune, and judge what's being
made according to what somebody did last week, to keep their job six months
longer.' And I said, 'If you do that, the music will always be the music, and
those son-of-a-bitches will never have any chance at it, you can make all the
money you want to, but they can't fuck with the music.' Paley said, 'That's very
interesting.' John walked out and said, 'You didn't want the job, did you?'"

whole; song by song the sound is not the same, but it is always a thing in itself. There is a glow that seems to come from inside the music. It's what Johnston called "that mountainside sound," and nothing explains that phrase as well as the final sound of "Like a Rolling Stone." As a single or on *Highway 61 Revisited*, mono or stereo, it has always sounded like Johnston to me.

"I don't remember, I don't remember," Johnston said when I asked him about the state of the master tape of "Like a Rolling Stone" when he took over Bob Dylan's recordings. "I got in there," he said after a while. "I would do anything I wanted to do and I never told anybody about anything. I never tried to jack anybody around—I would just go, and play, and say, 'Is this ok?' And that's how it happened. But as far as credit, as far as what I did with it, I really couldn't tell you."

I have always admired people who know how to interview. The key is not to want to be liked. The key is to be an irritant, a smart-aleck, a fool, a creep. "I heard your mother is a donkey," you might say, expecting the subject to spit in your face and walk out of the room. "*Oh, no,*" the person will say. "How did you ever get that idea? Let me tell you the *real* story. My mother is a *dolphin*. And how that happened, I've never told anyone . . ." One interviewer I know has a terrible stutter. People will say anything, will talk endlessly about their private lives, just to keep him from asking another question. The best I have ever been able to manage is silence.

"I think you spotted what it is," Johnston said finally. "I may have got in there and mixed that thing. I may have added to it. The thing that I tried to do—the first time I walked in with Dylan"—starting on 29 July 1965, for the first sessions for *Highway 61 Revisited* after "Like a Rolling Stone," cut more than a month earlier—"I said, 'Your voice has to come up.' He said, 'I don't like my voice, my voice is too god-damn loud.' And I'd say ok, and I'd turn it up a little bit, and he'd say"—and Johnston affects a clipped, effete voice—"'My voice is too *loud.*' Finally he quit saying that. My guess is he didn't want to fuck with me anymore, *but that's what I wanted.*"

"People were *fucking* with him. Wilson would fuck with him, *Do this, we gotta do that, this didn't come out.* Everything was wild and scattered, open, until I settled down on it, but that's the way that was."

Forty years after, anyone can be self-serving; anyone can gainsay the dead. But one sound can't gainsay another; you hear what you hear.

After "Like a Rolling Stone" was recorded Dylan took an acetate of the performance to Albert Grossman's house. Calls were made; people began to come by to hear the new sound. In the stories told of that night, you can almost smell the incense burning; there's something of the end of *Rosemary's Baby* in the scene, with the believers all gathered around Satan's bassinet and Ruth Gordon cooing, "The Child! Come see the Child!" The late Paul Rothchild had already produced the first recordings by the Paul Butterfield Blues Band, and less than two years later would produce the Doors' seven-minute "Light My Fire"; of all the stories emanating from that night, his may have aged the best. "I had them play the fucking thing five times straight before I could say anything," he told the Dylan biographer Bob Spitz. "What I realized while I was sitting there was that one of US—one of the so-called Village hipsters—was making music that could compete with THEM—the Beatles and the Stones and the Dave Clark Five—without sacrificing any of the integrity of folk music or the power of rock 'n' roll. As a producer, this was an awesome revelation for me. I knew the song was a smash, and yet I was consumed with envy because it was the best thing I'd heard any of our crowd do and I knew it was going to turn the tables on our nice, comfortable lives."

When the single was released, on 20 July 1965, copies serviced to radio stations cut the song in half and spread it over both sides of a red vinyl 45, giving them the option of airing only the first three minutes, thus preserving their normal song-to-commercial ratios. Dylan demanded that "Like a Rolling Stone" play through on its own side, and soon a new pressing replaced the first—but when the song first appeared on the radio, three minutes was all you heard, with the fade sounding fake, as if something was missing. When the word spread that something was, stations were hammered by callers demanding all six minutes, and six minutes was what they got. And then, it seemed, that was all your station played. If society did not raise itself as a single brave, terrified soul and leave itself behind, sometimes, listening to Dylan's voice as everything around him dropped away, as the demonic, despairing figure in the song threw off everything around itself, you could imagine that society had done just that. If people did not leave their homes to travel the roads making speeches and barbeque—though many did, and many already had—you could hear intimations of that, too. Or you could hear that event in its absence, as if, in its failure to instantly change the world, unlike any recording before it "Like a Rolling Stone" had proven that that was precisely what a work of art was supposed to do, and the standard by which a work of art should be judged. "When I heard 'Like a Rolling Stone,'" said Frank Zappa, in 1965 a twenty-four-year-old Los Angeles satirist who considered himself an anti-hippie, high-art, Edgard Varèse-meets-the-Penguins revolutionary, convinced that America was heading toward disaster if it wasn't already there, "I wanted to quit the music business, because I felt: 'If this wins and it does what it's supposed to do, I don't need to do anything else' . . . But it didn't do anything. It sold, but nobody responded to it the way that they should have." Younger people heard that their world was not quite as predictable as they might have thought. "What a shocking thing," said Elvis Costello, who as Declan MacManus turned eleven that summer, "to live in a world where there was Manfred Mann and the Supremes and Engelbert Humperdinck and here comes 'Like a Rolling Stone.'"

In a season where a Dylan composition was as close to a straight shot at the Top Ten as anything short of the next Beatles record—following the Byrds, whose first album contained three Dylan songs besides "Mr. Tambourine Man" and featured a photo of Dylan fronting the band (which already looked ridiculous in matching turtlenecks), the Turtles threatened to turn the enterprise into instant kitsch with Dylan's "It Ain't Me Babe"—there were cover versions of "Like a Rolling Stone." The Turtles, on their 1965 debut album, gave up after two verses. The Young Rascals, who despite their short pants and ruffles were at their best a devastating punk R&B band, put a full-length version on their own first album in 1966, with embarrassingly affected Dylanish vocals soon enough leavened by the singer's obvious fascination with the lyrics, great shouts of "C'mon!" to lead off the choruses, and an organ player who, following Al Kooper's extended chords, established that he could hold down a single key for the length of an entire verse.* "That's what happens when you ain't got no more money, baby," one of the Rascals announced at the end. "Beat it!" said another. The Beverly Hills combo Dino (son of Dean Martin), Desi (son of Desi Arnaz) and Billy (nobody

---

* "After the release of *Highway 61*, and the success of it," Kooper says, "there were times when Bob and I would go to a record store and buy the imitation records of it, and then go back to his place and listen and sit there and laugh. I was particularly amused by the fact that really great musicians were imitating my ignorance. I really had devoted my time to being a guitar player, and I was now just starting to play keyboards, for a living. I had so much to learn."

famous) did a preteen version—not to mention "Como una Piedra Rodante" for the Mexican market. No one noticed in the U.S.A., but in 1966 in Kingston, Jamaica, a rock-steady trio called the Wailers—Bob Marley, Peter Tosh, and Bunny Wailer—rewrote the song as "Rolling Stone" and resang it in the tone of an elder reading a child to sleep with a fable about the wages of sin. The chorus, led by Marley, was the same, but the single repeated verse put new blood on the song. "Nobody told you was to roam on the street," Bunny Wailer crooned sadly. "But that's what happens when you lie and cheat/ You have no nights and you have no mornings/ Time like scorpion stings without warning."

There were other covers. But more than anything there was talk, arguments over the words, people trying to learn the song on their own instruments, or their own voices, to find their own stories in the song and tell them: people singing along, in every way imaginable. One of them was the comedian and *Homicide/Special Victims Unit* detective Richard Belzer, who turned twenty-one the summer of 1965. "I think the very first time I saw you perform was on *Saturday Night Live*, and you were doing your impression of Bob Dylan in a retirement center, singing in a Yiddish accent," the interviewer Terry Gross said to Belzer twenty-two years later. "Right," Belzer said, "the eighty-six-year-old Bob Dylan." "I hate to ask questions like this, 'How did that idea come to you,'" Gross said, "but really, how did that idea come to you?" "Well," Belzer said, "when I was a *kid* . . ."

I hate to say that Bob is that much older than me, but when I was a *teenager*, and was first getting into Bob Dylan, then we found out his real name is *Zimmerman*, and he's a *Jew*, from *Minne*sohtaa, and this was like a *revelation*, to have a hero that's a *Jew*— So I said, if his name's Zimmerman, he must have had a bar mitzvah. So I fanta- sized what Bob Dylan's bar mitzvah must have been like. [In a clogged nasal voice] "Ah, Baruh Atah Ado*noi* Elohenu Meleh ha- *olam*, asher kidshanu b'mitzvo-*tah*—" And then he gets *older:* "Oy! Oy!" [In an especially cranky, clogged nasal voice] "Vonce upon a tame, ya dreshed so fine, ya t'rew da bums a dime in ya prime— [and then in a triumphantly I-told-you-so clogged nasal voice] DIDN'T YA! People call, shed b'ware doll ya bound ta fall, you t'ought dey was all, KIDDIN' YA!"

It's a great thing, when a song defines a summer, and like the Jamies' "Summertime, Summertime" in 1958 or Martha and the Vandellas' "Dancing in the Street" in 1964—which, as a theme song for the Watts riots, came back even more strongly after 11 August 1965—that was the first thing "Like a Rolling Stone" did. When school is out, when people are on vacation, when restraints are looser, when the weather is warm and people are living their lives in the open air, possi- bilities seem fuller, closer, and the possibilities lined out in "Like a Rolling Stone" were endless. Like a preacher, Dylan sang doom through the song; while no one missed the threat, the freedom the song defined as specifically as the Declara- tion of Independence, with nearly as strong an ear for cadence, overrode everything else. You could sing along, "No direction *home*," just like you sang along to "Satisfaction," or you could sing along like Richard Belzer or the Wailers, rewriting the song because, you knew, it was something more than a song, or anyway something else.

It was an event. It defined the summer, but like the Watts riots the performance also interrupted it—as, ever since, the song has interrupted whatever might be taking place around it as it plays.* It was an incident that took place in a record-

---

* "There's a very odd way to hear the song for the first time, I think," Paula Radice, an elementary school teacher in Hastings, England, said in 2004 in a modest, soft-spoken voice; she was one of several people interviewed for a BBC radio documentary on "Like a Rolling Stone," produced for the Birmingham series "Soul Music." "Because I came to Dylan late, and only encountered him in the 1980s, as opposed to all these people who've known the song since the sixties, it came to me completely fresh and completely new. I was sitting in a pub in Durham, in 1984, at about the time of the miners' strike, and Durham was a rather downbeat place at the time—people were out collecting in tins. It was a strange time to be at a fairly well-off university, in a very unhappy part of the world. And I was sitting in this pub, very old-fashioned type, non-studenty pub, so traditional in fact that I don't think they even served women at the bar. There was just a general hubbub of conversation. The jukebox was playing, and suddenly this song started. I didn't know what it was—I was probably the only person in the pub that didn't recognize it. But everything stopped. Everybody's conversation stopped, and everybody started singing. And I thought, what on earth is going on, I've never heard this song before, how come *everybody else* knows it? And not only did everybody else know it, they obviously *loved* it, and relished it, and were throwing their heads back singing the chorus, 'How does it feel,' really sort of howling it out. Looking back on it, it seems to me highly emblematic of what was going on in Durham at the time. There was a sort of vituperative elation in the song that they cottoned on to. At the end of the song, as if nothing had happened, everybody went back to drinking and talking."

ing studio and was then sent out into the world with the intention of leaving the world not quite the same. This is not the same as changing the world, which implies a way in which one might want the world to be changed. This is more like drawing a line, to see what would happen: to see who the song revealed to be on which side of the line, and who might cross it, from either side. In that way, the song as an event transformed its listeners into witnesses. It was up to the listeners-as-witnesses to make sense of what they saw and heard in the song, to tell the story to others, as Belzer did; to carry the event with them or to seek to leave it behind, as they wished, or as they could, because one's response to an event is not something anyone can entirely choose.

CHAPTER EIGHT

Three Stages

That event was taken to the country at large—the factual country, as it was in that noisy, murderous, idyllic summer of 1965, and the imagined country, as Dylan would map it on *Highway 61 Revisited*, which was released on August 30, just in time for everyone to go back to real life.

The first step was Dylan's performance at the Newport Folk Festival, where over the previous two years, surrounded by contemporary hit-makers like Joan Baez and Peter, Paul & Mary, legendary names from the founding blues and country records of the 1920s and '30s, among them Son House, Mother Maybelle Carter, Skip James, Roscoe Holcomb, Clarence Ashley, Mississippi John Hurt, and Dock Boggs, and such guardians of the tradition as the songster and ban-joist Pete Seeger and the folklorist Alan Lomax, he had emerged as the biggest draw and the most mystical presence. Dylan's friend Paul Nelson was at the time a critic for his own *Little Sandy Review* in Minneapolis and for *Sing Out!* the house organ of the folk movement; as he put it in 1975, posing as a private eye for the Watchtower Detective Agency and running down Dylan's biography for prospective clients "looking for a hero" to promote, "In the mid-Sixties Dylan's talent evoked such an intense degree of personal participation from both his admirers and detractors that he could not be permitted so much as a random action. Hungry for a sign, the world used to follow him around, just waiting for him to drop a cigarette butt. When he did they'd sift through the remains, looking for significance. The scary part is they'd find it."

Also at Newport in 1965 was the Paul Butterfield Blues Band, whose appearance as a white-led electric blues band led to a fight between Albert Grossman, who was managing them as well as Dylan and Peter, Paul & Mary, and Alan Lomax, who had introduced Butterfield's group on its own stage as a fraud and a joke. "I was cheering," Michael Bloomfield wrote in 1977. "I said, 'Kick that ass, Albert.'" Dylan asked Bloomfield to find him a band, and along with Al Kooper Bloomfield recruited drummer Sam Lay and bassist Jerome Arnold from the Butterfield band, and pianist Barry Goldberg. They rehearsed overnight; the next evening, on July 25, they took the stage. "I was wearing Levi's, a button-down shirt and a sports coat," Bloomfield said. "The black guys from the Butterfield Band were wearing gold shoes and had processes. Dylan wore rock and roll clothes: black leather jacket, yellow pin shirt without the tie. And he had a Fender Stratocaster. He looked like someone from *West Side Story*."

"The audience [was] booing and yelling 'get rid of the electric guitar,'" Nelson reported at the time. There were catcalls and screams and shouts and cheers. The band played a fierce "Maggie's Farm," with Bloomfield leading the way, and a clattering "Phantom Engineer," a song that would turn up under another title and in an entirely different mode on *Highway 61 Revisited*; in between was "Like a Rolling Stone," already all over the radio, which escaped from its creators. They couldn't find the song; it lumbered and groaned, until finally it fell back into its beginnings as a waltz and Dylan gave up singing the song and began declaiming it, as if it were a speech. As music it was a non-event; after Elvis Presley's third, above-the-waist appearance on the Ed Sullivan show, in 1957, and the Beatles' debut there in 1964, as a performance it has grown into perhaps the most storied event in the history of modern popular music.

It has since become weirdly fashionable to claim that there was no booing—or, if one admits that there was less-than-pleasant noise coming from the audience during and between the songs, at least no condemnation of Dylan's new music in that form. The sound was too loud, some say, and people, especially the elite of the folk movement, seated up front, who, the argument goes, were inexplicably familiar with the technical side of amplified music, were simply calling for a better mix. Or the sound was not loud enough. Or people in the back, misunderstanding the constructive criticism offered by the people in the front, and not wanting to appear uninformed, imitated what they mistakenly took to be boos and thus drowned out the helpful suggestions. Or people were booing because Dylan only played three songs, which is imaginable, though that doesn't account for people booing before the band finished and left. Or, as Geoff Muldaur has recently argued, people in the folk movement were booing because Bob Dylan was playing bad rock 'n' roll, and they knew good rock 'n' roll from bad and appreciated the former. Or, as David Hajdu implied in 2001 in his hagiography of the sixties novelist, Don Juan, and Dylan imitator Richard Fariña, the whole thing was a fraud cooked up after the fact by Dylan and his sycophants as a publicity stunt.

There was no controversy at the time as to whether or not the crowd booed Bob Dylan. The only controversy was over the music itself, and the controversy was not about whether it was good rock 'n' roll or bad rock 'n' roll. The music was the cigarette butt, and people made up their minds about its significance on the spot.

It was the first time the singer known for his vagabond's guitar and hobo harmonica had performed with a rock 'n' roll band since high school. One of his first original songs, written in Hibbing in 1958, was "Hey Little Richard," which can be heard in James Marsh's 1993 television documentary *Tales of Rock 'N' Roll: Highway 61 Revisited,* with a scratchy home tape of the tune running under an outside shot of what in 1958 was Dylan's second-floor room in the Zimmerman house, so that the song appears to be coming right out of the window. "Little Richard, oooooo, Little Richard," Dylan shouts, hammering a piano. "Little Richard gonna find it out—Little Richard." But Little Richard was not Woody Guthrie, Bob Dylan's first folk music hero, troubadour of the dispossessed, poet of the Great Depression, ghost of the American highway, a man blown by the wind and made out of dust. Little Richard, though he was for a time someone millions of people actually wanted to hear, was not Of the People; Little Richard was a freak, a foot of pomade, a pound of makeup, and purple clothes. Little Richard was rock 'n' roll, and in 1961, when Bob Dylan would offer the scenemakers in Village folk clubs sneering parodies of doo-wop and teenage laments ("I'm gonna kill my parents," he burbled in "Acne," as Ramblin' Jack Elliott supplied backing doo-wahs, "because they don't understand")—or in 1964, when at his Halloween concert at Philharmonic Hall Dylan pretended he didn't know "Leader of the Pack" was by the Shangri-Las and not the Marvelettes, since obviously anything in the Top 40 was interchangeable with anything else—or in 1965, to some of the people in the crowd at Newport, rock 'n' roll was pandering to the crowd, cheapening everything that was good in yourself by selling yourself to the highest bidder, putting advertising slogans on your back if that's what it took. "To

the folk community," said Bloomfield, who had been part of
it, "rock 'n' roll was greasers, heads, dancers, people who got
drunk and boogied. Lightnin' Hopkins had made electric
records for twelve years, but he didn't bring his electric band
from Texas. No, sir, he came out at Newport like they had
just taken him out of the fields, like the tar baby."

Promising an acoustic guitar, and nobody else, Peter
Yarrow of Peter, Paul & Mary got the audience to call Dylan
back to the stage. He sang "Mr. Tambourine Man" and "It's All
Over Now, Baby Blue"—"a song," Nelson wrote, "that I took
to be his farewell to Newport," and in fact Bob Dylan would
not appear there again for thirty-seven years.* "In penance—
in penance!—Dylan put on his old Martin and played,"
Bloomfield said in 1977, his disgust as full as it was twelve
years before. "Dylan should have just given them the finger."

---

* "The thing that was most apparent to me was how ghostly it was," the historian Sean Wilentz wrote me about the festival in 2002, "—because they're all
dead. All the people the young folk artists were drawn to in 1965 or before.
Mississippi John Hurt is dead. Son House is dead ... There were a lot of
ghosts around. At the same time it was a very conscious passing on of that tradition to something new—on the part of the older folks. Dylan did that very
intentionally. Songs that he was singing in 1965, and songs that recalled that
tradition.

"There was a roots stage—but given the explosion of interest in old-time
music, there was too little of it. Most of the music was personal song-stories.
What with *O Brother, Where Art Thou?* Alison Krauss, the festival seemed to be
out of step with where folk music now *is*. It was largely virtuoso self-indulgent
adolescent angst. It was Shawn Colvin.

"Dylan walked out on stage with Jewish earlocks—and a ponytail, and a
fake beard. He looked like a guy who was on the bus to [the Hasidic Brooklyn

Five days later, on July 29, Dylan returned to the studio, with Russ Savakus and Al Kooper's friend Harvey Goldstein (later Harvey Brooks) replacing Joe Macho, Jr., on bass, and Bob Johnston producing, over the next few days Dylan recorded the rest of *Highway 61 Revisited*, including the eleven-minute "Desolation Row"—which Johnston took as Dylan's reply to his enemies at Newport—and his next single, "Positively 4th Street," which nearly everybody took to be his response to his enemies at Newport, especially Greenwich Village flatterers and hypocrites who, the singer said pityingly, "just want to be on the side that's winning," though people in Minnesota have always believed it was about 4th Street in Minneapolis.

Newport forced people to take sides—or allowed them the thrill of taking sides. What you hear from the crowd at Dylan's next show, at the Forest Hills Tennis Stadium on Long Island—his first full-scale debut of his new music—are people who have come together to fight a cultural war.

[*continued*] neighborhood] Crown Heights and got lost. From another angle, not really seeing the beard, he could have been in the Shangri-Las. Then he looked like Jesus Christ. He was putting on a show, and he was donning a mask—because he's a minstrel. A Jewish minstrel. An American minstrel.

"There came a point when he could have said something [about what had happened in 1965]—when he was introducing the band. I looked at him very closely then—but he just sort of smiled. He twitched. And then he went into the last song, 'Leopard-skin Pill-box Hat.' Then he does a sizzling Buddy Holly, 'Not Fade Away.' Again it was ghosts. He was the whole fucking tradition. He was a one-man festival."

Dylan had put together a new band; in addition to Goldstein on bass and Kooper on electric piano, there was Robbie
Robertson on guitar and Levon Helm on drums, the latter
two from Levon and the Hawks, the barnstorming bar band
from Toronto. The ensemble would accompany Dylan for
one more show, at the Hollywood Bowl on September 3.
After that the rest of the Hawks—pianist Richard Manuel,
organist Garth Hudson, and bassist Rick Danko—joined
Robertson and Helm, and with them around him Dylan set
out across the country. In the fall Helm left in despair over
the rancor the band encountered, over audiences enraged by
the turn of a folk singer whose words you could understand
toward a sound so big it demanded you surrender one kind of
meaning for another; other drummers, lastly and most
notably Mickey Jones, took his place until the group dis-
banded when their long tour, which took them back and
forth across the United States, to Australia, to Scandinavia,
to Ireland, and up and down England and Scotland, ended in
London in the late spring of 1966. After that Dylan had his
famous motorcycle accident and quit the road. In Woodstock, he played possum, and began to look for new music.
He appeared occasionally over the next years with the
Hawks, by 1968 renamed as the Band, with Helm again part
of the group. He did not tour again for eight years.

At Forest Hills Dylan's show was presented in the form it
would keep for the next eight months: a solo acoustic performance, a break, and then a return with the band. New fans

of Dylan's Top 40 hits were there, and Top 40 disc jockeys introduced both sets; Dylan could not have been more provocative if he had appeared for the second part of the show riding in a solid-gold Eldorado, or for that matter on a golden calf, and people were ready to be provoked. The crowd was with Dylan all the way for the acoustic half of the show, instantly catching the rhythm and the refrain of the still-unreleased, never-before-played "Desolation Row," laughing at the tricksters in the song as Cinderella turned into Bette Davis and Einstein traded clothes with Robin Hood. There were no formal protest songs, nothing from *The Freewheelin' Bob Dylan* or *The Times They Are A-Changin'*, no "With God on Our Side" or "A Hard Rain's A-Gonna Fall," but the troubadour was present and true, and the crowd cheered.*

When Dylan came back with the band, for "Maggie's Farm," an electric "It Ain't Me Babe," from the 1964 acoustic album *Another Side of Bob Dylan*, and more songs that would appear on *Highway 61 Revisited*, again and again fury coursed through the crowd like a snake; the wails of hate are beyond belief. Listening now, you can feel a mass of people bucking and weaving, many of them as united in their screaming as twelve-year-old female Beatle fans were with theirs—"Okay,

---

* Even in 1974, when Dylan and the Band once again toured the country, the segment of the show that featured Dylan alone, accompanied only by his own acoustic guitar and harmonica, almost always brought the most ecstatic response, with many cheering and applauding with such fervor they were enacting a rejection of everything else that was played.

when he goes 'band,' we all go PAUL!" except that at Forest Hills it could be "Okay, right now, all together, SCUMBAG!" The performance is a screech; the musicians flay at the songs. "Like a Rolling Stone" came last. While here the cheers now outnumbered the boos—this was, for many, the reason they were there—you can hear both Dylan and the band pull back from the song, from its difficulty, its elusive shape, from the challenge, it turned out, that the song embodied not only for whoever heard it, but anyone who thought he or she could play it. By the end, with only Kooper, with his electric piano, seemingly willing to take responsibility for the monster, the song seemed reduced to one repeating plinking note.

Six days later in Hollywood, there was far less booing—though the only person I have ever met who has admitted to booing Bob Dylan in 1965, and perhaps the only person alive willing to admit it, did it at the Hollywood Bowl—but the sound of the ensemble had devolved toward whatever the radio was sounding like, and "Like a Rolling Stone" was still a fish story. Shirley Poston, writing in *The Beat*, the radio station newsletter that for all of its embarrassments (even in 1965, most Top 40 listeners probably knew that Eric Burdon of the Animals was not "the greatest blues singer in the world") was at the time as good as any other pop music publication available, tells the story best.

This was the moment the majority of the audience had been waiting for. Dylan, in the flesh, singing the number one song that has made him the idol of millions instead of just thousands.

It was probably the moment he'd been waiting for, too.

He knew the song by heart. So did his audience. Unfortunately, the band did not. And the famous "Like a Rolling Stone" was minus the powerful Dylan composed background that helped catapult the song and the singer to international fame.

But Dylan made the best of it. There hadn't been time for the band to learn the intricate arrangement, so the band just more or less played on.

Soon enough, in Texas, Dylan would chase the song with the Hawks. Over the next months, their music grew in power and ambition. It seemed that nothing was beyond their grasp—but "Like a Rolling Stone" remained out of reach. The country they were traversing was, somehow, giving back less than the country Dylan had already explored on *Highway 61 Revisited*.

CHAPTER NINE

Democracy in America

This may be the truest setting for "Like a Rolling Stone"—a country imagined forty years ago, and as recognizable today as it was then.

U.S. Highway 61 runs from the Gulf of Mexico to the Canadian border, just above Grand Portage, Minnesota. In Dylan's high school days in Hibbing it was a magic road; he and his friends would cut twenty miles east for a straight shot down U.S. 53 to Duluth, where he was born, and there they'd pick up 61 and head for St. Paul and Minneapolis, looking for scenes;* in 1959 and 1960, when Dylan attended

---

* In Minnesota the driving age was fifteen; Dylan made his first recordings at Terline Music, an instrument and sheet music store, in St. Paul on Christmas Eve, 1956. Included were fragments of Little Richard's "Ready Teddy," Sonny Knight's "Confidential" (a song Dylan took up again in 1967 with the Hawks,

the University of Minnesota, the highway took him to his haunts. In the Cities Dylan discovered folk music, the old country music and the old blues—and discovered that in song and story there was no more protean line drawn in the nation than the line drawn by Highway 61. History had been made on that highway in times past, and history would be made there in times to come.

Bessie Smith, the Queen of the Blues, died on Highway 61 in 1937, near Clarksdale, Mississippi, where Muddy Waters grew up and where, in the 1910s and '20s, Charley Patton, Son House, and others made the Delta blues; some have pretended to know that Robert Johnson's 1936 "Cross Road Blues" was set right there, where Highway 49 crosses Highway 61. Elvis Presley grew up on Highway 61, in the Lauderdale Courts public housing in Memphis; not far away, the road went past the Lorraine Motel, where Martin Luther

---

[*continued*] as part of the Basement Tapes recordings, and was still performing on stage twenty-five years after that), Carl Perkins's "Boppin' the Blues," Lloyd Price's "Lawdy Miss Clawdy," the Five Satins' "In the Still of the Nite," Shirley and Lee's "Let the Good Times Roll," and the Penguins' "Earth Angel." Dylan accompanied himself on piano; friends Howard Rutman and Larry Keegan also sang. Left a paraplegic after accidents in his teens and twenties, Keegan, in his wheelchair, joined Dylan onstage in Merrillville, Indiana, in 1981, for an encore of Chuck Berry's "No Money Down" (Dylan played saxophone), and in 1999 sang at Jesse Ventura's inauguration as governor of Minnesota. Keegan died in 2001 of a heart attack, at fifty-nine; he had always kept the aluminum disc that resulted from the 1956 session, and after his death relatives listed it on eBay, supposedly with a $150,000 floor, though no bid close to that was forthcoming. "Awful," says one sympathetic listener who heard the songs.

King was shot in 1968. "Highway 61, go right past my baby's door," goes the blues that has been passed from hand to hand since the highway took its name. "I walked Highway 61, 'til I gave out at my knees," sang John Wesdon in 1993. The highway doesn't give out; from Hibbing, it would have seemed to go to the ends of the earth, carrying the oldest strains of American music along with businessmen and escaped cons, vacationers and joy-riders blasting the radio—carrying runaway slaves north, before the long highway had a single name, and, not so much more than a century later, carrying Freedom Riders south. Highway 61 embodies an America as mythical and real as the America made up in Paris out of old blues and jazz records by the South American expatriates in Julio Cortázar's 1963 novel *Hopscotch*—a novel which, like a highway, you can enter wherever you choose, and go backward or forward any time you like.

Most people who bought Bob Dylan's *Highway 61 Revisited* in 1965 had probably never heard of the road the album was named for; today the record is as much a part of the lore of the highway as anything else. The album cover, as with *Bringing It All Back Home* a photograph by Daniel Kramer, pictured two people ready for a journey: Dylan, sitting on a sidewalk in a gaudy pink, blue, and purple shirt open over a Triumph Motorcycles T-shirt and holding a pair of sunglasses in his right hand; and a second man, standing behind Dylan, visible only from the waist down, in jeans and a horizontally striped orange and white T-shirt, his right thumb hooked into his pants pocket with a camera hanging from his clutched fingers, and the viewer's eye directed straight at his crotch. I remember a college friend bringing the album home as a present for his younger brother; his mother took one look at the thing and threw it out of the house.

The journey described on the album took in the country. When you hear "Like a Rolling Stone" as a single, the story it tells takes place wherever you happen to hear it; on *Highway 61 Revisited*, it was a flight from New York City. One step across the city line, with "Tombstone Blues," you were in Tombstone, Arizona, without Wyatt Earp—or Levittown, or Kansas City, any town or suburb in the nation, where people talked about money and school, losing their virginity and the war in Vietnam, dreamed about sex and the west, about Belle Starr and Ma Rainey, and the president damned them all. Cutting hard around the turn of the song as it ended, Bloomfield led the charge out of town; then the road took over, and while anything could happen on it, there was nothing happening outside of it. The road was a reverie, movement on this highway as peaceful, as slow-rocking as a cradle in "It Takes a Lot to Laugh, It Takes a Train to Cry," a timeless blues with a timeless, commonplace verse at its center, a woman at the end, Dylan singing the song of an unworried man and the band blowing behind him like a breeze—

> Don't the moon look good, mama
> Shinin' through the trees?

—and the road was a crackup, the singer shouting out the window as he sped past the carnage in "From a Buick 6." The band is trying to get out of there as fast as he is, taking the turns too fast, as if there is such a thing as too fast when you can't get the blood out of your mind, when, as Dylan sang, in words that were suddenly about anything—films of what Allied forces found in Nazi extermination camps in 1945, as seen by American school children in the late 1940s and early '50s, as the historian Robert Cantwell has suggested, or news footage, just beginning to appear on American television, of dead Vietnamese and U.S. Army body bags, as anyone could have thought, or just the wreck on the highway—you "need a steam shovel, mama, to keep away the dead."

In "Ballad of a Thin Man," the travelers have circled back to New York. In a back room in a bar you're better off not knowing too much about, someone who thought he belonged anywhere is finding out what nowhere means. The piano rolling the tune into place is so ominous it's one step short of a cartoon starring Snidely Whiplash; then Snidely Whiplash is Peter Lorre in *M*. On the highway, there is a strange place every ten miles, somewhere where nobody knows you and nobody cares, and no one is cool; in New York City, the singer is a hipster, snapping his fingers, and as he does a whole cast of grotesques appears to point and taunt, to see if the mark can escape from the locked room. Then the album turns over, into "Queen Jane Approximately," and the singer rides the wheels of the music on his back, swimming in his own sound, as he reaches for a woman who, like the girl in the song that started the tale, seemingly a long, long time ago, has nowhere to go. It was one of many mid-to-late sixties songs on the soundtrack of Bernardo Bertolucci's *The Dreamers*, his 2004 movie about three young people making their own world out of sex, movies, and parental allowances in a Paris apartment, as, outside their windows, the near-revolution of May 1968 took place in the streets. There was Jimi Hendrix, the Doors, the Grateful Dead. "It's not fair, to put them up against something from that album," a friend said. Then "Highway 61 Revisited," with Dylan squeezing a police-car siren in what is probably his most perfectly written song, sung as the ultimate tall tale. You find out that not only can anything happen on Highway 61—a father murdering his son, a mother sleeping with one of hers, the Gross National Product dumped as landfill or World War III staged as a stock car race, in other words Bessie Smith killed in a car crash, Gladys Presley walking a teenage Elvis to school, or Martin Luther King lying dead on a balcony—it already has. As the song plays, the band chasing a rockabilly rabbit, the singer snarling with glee, the road goes in every direction at once, and then it is one of the tornadoes that sweeps down from Fargo to Minneapolis, picking up cars and dropping them off the map. In "Just Like Tom Thumb's Blues," the singer turns up in Juárez, Mexico, and all he wants is out. He's seen the country east and west, north and south, most importantly backward and forward. "I'm going back to New York City," he says, understanding that the joke he tried to tell the country is on him. "I do believe I've had enough." But there is one more song.

"Desolation Row," Al Kooper wrote in 1998, was on Eighth Avenue in New York City, "an area infested with whore houses, sleazy bars, and porno-supermarkets totally beyond renovation or redemption." At the time it was the kind of place where you were told to walk down the middle of the street if you were stuck there at night, because you were better off with the drivers who didn't see you than with the people on the sidewalks who did. But even more than "Just Like Tom Thumb's Blues," the eleven-minute song has a south-of-the-border feeling, and not just because the work by the Nashville session guitarist Charlie McCoy, brought in by Bob Johnston, reaches back to Marty Robbins's 1959 cowboy ballad "El Paso." In the U.S.A. Mexico is a place you run to.

You are walking down the middle of Eighth Avenue, trying not to look at the neon lights above the street and the unlit doorways on either side of it. As it is on Eighth Avenue, culture in "Desolation Row" is the scrapheap of Western civilization, decay at best and betrayal at worst, and by now, at the end of Highway 61, you can find culture anywhere, in a beauty parlor, in a police station, on a bed, in a doctor's office, at a carnival, on the *Titanic* as it sinks. Dylan follows his characters through the song as if he is the detective and they are the suspects; what he learns is that almost no one keeps what she has, and that almost everyone sells his birthright for a mess of pottage. The song, Dylan once said, was his "America the Beautiful," and he sings the song dead-pan, which is part of why it is so funny; the scrapheap gives off a sickening but intoxicating smell of missed chances, folly, error, narcissism, sin. Everything seems worthless. In the theater, you're laughing, but when the show is over, as the Russian philosopher Vasily Rozanov once wrote, you turn around to get your coat out of the coatroom and go home: "No more coats and no more home." "Desolation Row" seems merely to give the scrapheap a name—except that in Dylan's guided tour of the place, with Cinderella making a home in Desolation Row, Casanova punished for visiting it, Ophelia not being allowed in, it becomes plain that the scrapheap is also a utopia. It's a nowhere described again, in more ordinary language, as a chronicle of more ordinary events, in "Visions of Johanna," a song from *Blonde on Blonde*, from the late spring of 1966, though under the title "Seems Like a Freeze-Out" Dylan was already performing it on stage in the fall of 1965, just after *Highway 61 Revisited* was released.

Here Desolation Row could very easily be an apartment on Eighth Avenue, somewhere well above the street, with the singer looking out the window. The song makes a dank room where a draft just blows balls of dust across the floor. In the corners some people are having sex; others are shooting up or nodding out. It's a bohemian paradise, a place of with-drawal, isolation, and gloom. It's fourth-hand Poe, third-hand Baudelaire, passed down by the countless people who've bought into the fable of the artist who cannot be understood, the visionary whom society must exile for its own protection—must exile within itself, so that his or her humiliation is complete and final, but that's the danger. That's the one card left to the artist, and with that card the artist can change the game. As Dylan does on *Highway 61 Revisited*, from one end of the highway to the other, stopping at every spot that looks like it might have the best cheeseburger on the strip or for that matter the worst, the artist will return society's vitriol with mockery and scorn of his or her own. The difference is that while society speaks only in shibboleths and clichés, the artist invents a new language. When society's language has been forgotten, people will still be trying to learn the artist's language, to speak as strangely, with such indecipherable power. That's the idea.

The dank room where this magic is made is its own cliché, of course, but there's nowhere else the singer in "Desolation Row," or anyone else in the song who's allowed in and allowed to remain, would rather be. All of them, the Good Samaritan, Casanova, Einstein back when he used to play the electric violin, Cinderella—well, actually that's it, along with the singer those are the only people named who've left traces in the place, and Casanova's gone—stick their heads out the window, eyeballing those few they might judge worthy of joining them, laughing down at the crowds on the street, at all those who don't know enough to beg to be let in. They watch the horrors taking place in the building across the street, where the Phantom of the Opera is about to serve a meal of human flesh, but it's nothing they haven't seen before; why do you think they're here and not there? The voice in "Desolation Row" and "Visions of Johanna" is partly Jack Kerouac's voice, in his narration for Robert Frank and Alfred Leslie's 1959 life-among-the-beatniks movie *Pull My Daisy*. "Look at all those cars out there," he says. "Nothing there but a million screaming ninety-year-old men being run over by gasoline trucks. So throw a match on it." From Kerouac you can go back more than half a century, and hundreds of years from there, and find yourself in the same room. In the Belgian painter James Ensor's 1885 *Scandalized Masks*, a man sits at a desk, a bottle before him, hat on his head and a pig-snout mask on his face. A woman stands in a doorway, holding a staff, a pointed hat on her head, black glasses over her eyes. Her nose is huge and bulbous, her chin sticks out like a growth; you can't tell if she's wearing a mask or if you're looking at her face. Yes, it's Brussels, they're just going to Mardi Gras—but at the same time, in this sadistically prosaic scene, you know something unspeakable is going to happen as soon as the two leave the chamber. You know the carnival they're going to is not in the public streets but on Desolation Row, that place where the old heretics, the witches, the ancestors of the bohemians of the modern world, perform their ceremonies.

That is where "Desolation Row" almost leaves you. And then, eight and a half minutes into the song, with nine verses finished and one to go, Dylan and McCoy begin to hammer at each other with their guitars, and after more than a minute—with Dylan running a searing harmonica solo over the guitar playing, taking the song away from its form as a nonsensical folk ballad, as a "Froggy Went A-Courtin'" with its mice and ants and cats and snakes now dressed up by the MGM costume department—Dylan snaps the song into its last verse with three harsh, percussive bangs on his acoustic guitar, and the circle is complete. In this moment the song opens back into the sound of "Like a Rolling Stone," all threat, all promise, all demand. Once again it is time to get out of this suffocating room and onto Highway 61. Because all across *Highway 61 Revisited*, "Like a Rolling Stone" has hung in the air, like a cloud in the desert, beckoning. The song has taken you out into the country, so that you might see it for what it is, but also so that, caught up in the momentum of "Like a Rolling Stone," the thrill of its explosion, you might realize that the territory you have covered is also the country as it was. "Like a Rolling Stone" promises a new country; now all you have to do is find it. The engine is running; the tank is full.

CHAPTER TEN

Swinging London

Luckily for Bob Dylan, if he had one foot in the heretic's chamber, the bohemian's garret, the privileged slum of Desolation Row, as a pop musician, which by the summer and fall of 1965 he had so glamorously become—appearing on stage in a Carnaby Street–styled checked suit that made him over into a medieval court jester, or in a black shirt that, covered with huge white polka dots, signified that life was a joke and his mission was to tell it—his other foot was on the stairway of a plane.* With the Hawks he traveled the country as if he

---

* "I didn't give a fuck about Electric Bob or Folk Bob, and I didn't know anyone who did," the singer Bob Geldof wrote in 2003 of his thirteen-year-old self in Dublin in 1965. "It was the words, the voice, the shirt. I couldn't find one like it, so I painted spots on my blue shirt collar, the shoulders, and halfway down the front and didn't take my jacket off. One night I forgot and the girl who became the song 'Mary of the 4th Form' said I was tragic and told her friends."

were running for president. From September through March
they went from one coast to another four times, heading as
far north as Canada, as far south as Atlanta and Miami Beach.
Then in April—when Bobby Gregg and Sandy Konikoff,
who had replaced Levon Helm on drums, were themselves
replaced by Mickey Jones, formerly the drummer in Trini
Lopez's band, the big beat behind "If I Had a Hammer"—
they crossed the International Date Line. They carried the
country with them; the drama they enacted was no more or
less American than Coca-Cola or Mickey Mouse, Charlie
Chaplin or the Vietnam War. They played their last show on
27 May 1966, and it took them almost until then to get their
arms around "Like a Rolling Stone."

Bob Johnston was in the U.K. to record that final performance, and the concerts in Liverpool and Sheffield.
He remembers an incident that took place that last night
when, before the show began, with the curtain down, Dylan
came on stage to warm up. "I always just hung around the
curtains," Johnston says, "and he said, 'I think I'll play something on the piano.'" But the stage wasn't empty; to squeeze
in every last ticket, the promoters had ringed the stage itself
with seats.

They had about a hundred people sitting on the stage—they had
to get them all in the theater. People sitting on the stage—and this
one guy says, "As soon as he gets over here, and touches that
piano, I'm gonna knock the shit out of him." Dylan says, "You hear

that?" I said, "Yeah, come on over here, don't worry about it, let me sit on the piano bench." So I sit on the piano bench, looking at this guy, and I say [politely], "Look—I can do it myself, but I've got about fifteen people who are ready to put your ass in the hospital, or the morgue, whichever you would prefer. So if you open your mouth, while this is going on, you're gone to one or the other place, either the hospital or the fucking morgue."

"You can't tell when the booing's going to come up," Dylan said in San Francisco the previous December. "Can't tell at all. It comes up in the weirdest, strangest places, and when it does it's quite a thing in itself." But in Britain the sort of protests that had followed Dylan and the Hawks around the U.S.A. were organized. In the U.K. the Communist Party had long operated a network of Stalinist folk clubs, where what songs could be sung, who could sing what, and in what manner, was strictly controlled. The idea was to preserve the image of the folk, where, as in that theatre-in-the-round in the field in New Jersey where Joan Baez brought out Bob Dylan, the gathered community, reenacting what the historian Georgina Boyes calls "the imagined village," shared the same land, speech, and values. Pop music symbolized the destruction of that community by capitalist mass society, where all land was divided, speech was class, where there were no values and the Beatles were a commodity fetish.

Along with fans of Bob Dylan who were now disappointed, or confused, or angry over his new music, people were recruited out of the folk clubs to come to his shows and break them up; in other words, people paid to leave. When Dylan finished the first half of his shows, playing by himself—when, people have said again and again, the audience, "in reverence," did not stir, did not whisper, afraid to miss a word or an inflection—and then returned with the band, there were group walkouts and foot-stomping. There were banners unfurled and signs raised. There were cheers and applause, curses and cheers for the curses. In Sheffield, a bomb threat was phoned in to the hall. People in the crowds tried to shout each other down. There was unison slow clapping to throw the musicians off their timing, or to make a noise too big for even their own noise to overcome. Songs were stopped, sometimes for long moments; Dylan talked his way out of the crowd's refusals, or with the Hawks would play a false start, throw off the hand-clappers in turn, and then dash for the song before anyone had a chance to strike back. "Like a Rolling Stone" was always the last song, and on most nights the musicians had to fight their way to it; sometimes, when they got there, in the middle of the song, when it was flying under its own power, a machine that would keep going whether the musicians kept playing or not, Dylan would take his hands from his Stratocaster and flutter them around his mouth, then cup his hands like a megaphone and scream through his fingers, giving each word its own body. "When I would crack my snare drum," Mickey Jones says, "it was like a cannon going off. I played with a heavy right foot—I used to tell people, like a 105 howitzer. But you know what? Because of that right foot, and Rick Danko's beat, we worked together." No matter how well Bob Dylan and the Hawks played in the United States, no matter how fiercely, compared to the music sparked by the conflict in the U.K. it was barbershop harmony in a rowboat.

"They're all poets," Dylan said from the stage of the Royal Albert Hall in London, just before he began the song on May 27, introducing the band, sounding as if he were parodying what a singer stoned to his toenails would sound like, offering a final provocation, one last *good luck*. "This song here is dedicated to the Taj Mahal," he said sensibly enough, since there are ways in which "Like a Rolling Stone" is like the Taj Mahal. "We're going to leave after this song, and I want to say good-bye to all of you people, you've been very warm, great people, I-I-I-I, you know, you've been very nice people. I mean, here you are, sitting in this great huge place"—the crowd applauds heartily—"and," he says, his mush-mouthed voice suddenly a snake's tongue, focused on a single point, the venom pure sarcasm, "believe me, we've enjoyed *every minute* of being here." Their entry into the song is slow and grand, with a huge, shimmering sound from Jones's cymbals, and then the opening lines, ragged, furious, bitter. At the end the song falls apart, falls on the singer and the band, but there is tremendous applause.

That performance of the song, Johnston says, "is the best I ever heard in my life. Because he was angry, they were screaming at him—he said, *Fuck those people, let's play this thing*."

He didn't tell 'em what it was, he just started it. I came unglued—
once those magic things happen, you know it. And that was one of
'em. You can put that together with Jimi Hendrix and "The Star-
Spangled Banner." It's a revelation to put them together.

Dylan had been cheered for so long, and revered for so long—
all of a sudden he's out there and they're booing him. He said [in a
pinched, nasal voice], *You people don't know what rawk and rowl is, you
don't know anything about rawk and rowl, we invented rock and roll in America,
and if you'll listen to it*— He just kept getting madder and madder.

Ten days before the last show, at the Free Trade Hall in
Manchester on May 17, there was everything there was anywhere else in the U.K. and more of it. Because of that—
because of the tension between the people on the stage and
the shouters and clappers strategically spread out in pockets
throughout the theater—the result was likely the greatest
rock 'n' roll show ever played. It came to a head when it had
to, in a pause between "Ballad of a Thin Man"—which had
opened with a blues chord from Robbie Robertson so huge
you could imagine it raising the dead, or turning the living to
stone—and "Like a Rolling Stone," but not in a form that
Dylan, in his worst thoughts, could have expected.

"Judas!" shouted a young man.

"In many a dark hour/ I've been thinkin' about this/ That
Jesus Christ/ Was betrayed by a kiss." So Dylan had sung on
The Times They Are A-Changin': "But I can't think for you/ You'll
have to decide/ Whether Judas Iscariot/ Had God on his

side." Who stands up in a crowded theater and shouts "Judas!"
at a Jew? "Why'd you do it, Keith?" the radio producer Andy
Kershaw asked the late Keith Butler in 1999, in a tone
straight out of a 1950s cop show, a detective pushing a sus-
pect to confess that he killed his wife.

There was laughter, then cheers and applause, from
nowhere near the whole of the house. The Hawks try to start
the song. "I don't believe you," Dylan says finally, the contempt in his voice enough to suck water out of the ground.
Then he was inflamed: "You're a liar!" The musicians again try
to push him toward the music, and he turns to them, speaking flatly, like an officer taking his troops out of their
trenches: "Play fucking loud." Butler got up and left. "He's a
traitor," he told D. A. Pennebaker's film crew in the foyer.
"He wants shooting."

"In your face," Mickey Jones remembers. Garth Hudson
sends out a chord from his organ, and you can hear it vibrate;
Rick Danko's bass is bigger than the hall, bigger than the
town. The band rings Chuck Berry's bell; then from nearly
two hundred miles away it rings every bell in St. Paul's.

Dylan shoulders the song as if he has never felt such a
burden in his life—not the song, but everything that has
come before it, and the struggle that remains. It's a tiredness
beyond the body, a state of being; it turns into regret. Then
all emotions are possible; as it was when the song was
recorded, anything can be said. This time it is the fourth and
last chorus that takes the roof off the building, that blows out

all the limits of the song, with what at first seems like anger changing inside each word to an embrace, then revulsion, then awe, the singer himself agog at what comes next. Robbie Robertson plays out the string of the song for nearly another minute, as if refusing to let anyone leave; when he finished, applause drowned out whatever other noise there might have been.

"I'll never forget the look on Dylan's face," Malcolm Metcalfe said in 1999. He had arrived too late to buy a ticket to the sold-out show, so he and a friend sneaked in through a side door, wandering through passageways until they reached a door near the wings of the stage, where they listened to "Like a Rolling Stone." Then the door flew back and two men all but pulled the singer off his feet and out of the theater. "He looked as if he'd been in a car crash—somebody totally shocked."

CHAPTER ELEVEN

One More Time

The song was never the same after England; neither was Bob Dylan, and neither was his audience. He and the audience changed over the years, but except for stray moments the song had gone as far as people playing it could take it—or as far as it could take whoever tried to play it. "It's like a ghost is writing a song like that," Dylan said in 2004 of "Like a Rolling Stone," talking to Robert Hilburn of the Los Angeles *Times*. "It gives you the song and then it goes away, it goes away." On stage in the years to come, the song was itself the ghost. It wasn't the singer who got to decide to sing the song; the song decided.

The record stayed the same, which is to say that it remained unstable, that it was never the same. On stage in the years to come "Like a Rolling Stone" was all too often the same: a warhorse, trotted out one more time to circle the track. It could seem longer each time you heard it played, as if the struggle had changed from getting to the song to getting out of it. Often the music thinned, and the song was like a bad bluegrass tune; often it was pumped up, and then a certain thrill came out of the lifts and rises in the rhythm, no matter what else was missing. There was a night in 1992, on a show marking the tenth anniversary of *Late Night with David Letterman* on NBC, with Letterman wearing what looked like Carl Perkins's toupee and Dylan fronting not only the house band but guitarists Chrissie Hynde and Steve Vai (who, after standing in for the Devil in *Crossroads*, an embarrassing 1986 Walter Hill movie about a lost Robert Johnson song, was clearly delighted to be on the side of the angels), a gorgeous Carole King on piano, and backing singers Mavis Staples, Rosanne Cash, Emmylou Harris, Michelle Shocked, and Nancy Griffith, who didn't come in until the third chorus, when Staples took the lead from Dylan. It was one of those times when anything he sang sounded like "One Hundred Bottles of Beer on the Wall." It's exciting to watch the performance today—to see the song sing itself, even if, as it does so, it refers back only to what Dylan once did with it. There have been a thousand performances where the same nothing happens, with more flair or less, but no real difference.

Other people continued to sing the song. In 1990, the Replacements, the Twin Cities' most confused and beloved punk band, wasted three pained minutes on the first half, with leader Paul Westerberg chewing over the words, the band trying to trash the chords, as if "Like a Rolling Stone," for the moment retitled "Like a Rolling Pin," was a great, rotting corpse, and also their true legacy, something they could no more deny than they could shed their own skin, though they had already spent years trying to do just that. In 2001, on *Duluth Does Dylan*, a birthplace tribute album marking Dylan's sixtieth birthday, the addled surf band the Black Labels (what, you don't think they have surfing on Lake Superior?) offered their version of "Rainy Day Women #12 & 35," Dylan's number 2 single from *Blonde on Blonde.* "Everybody must get stoned, like a *rolling* stone," they insisted, and why hadn't anyone thought of that before? On a 1995 album recorded in small clubs, even the Rolling Stones finally accepted the old dare; Dylan joined them onstage that year, and he and Mick Jagger passed the number back and forth as if exchanging trademarks. But except on the rarest occasions, the song did not happen; it didn't sweep up time and start a story for the first time. One night that it did was during Dylan's two-week stand at the Warfield Theatre in San Francisco in 1980. It was November 12, three days before Michael Bloomfield would appear to play the song, and this time it flew.

There is a certain delirium the song can grant whoever plays it; restaging the entire 1966 Manchester concert in 1996 at the Borderline Club in London, the singer Robyn Hitchcock, then in his early forties, found it in spades. Everyone had a part to play, especially the audience; someone shouts "Judas!" at the wrong time. Then at the right moment several people shout it, and just like that, Hitchcock's band, each member impersonating a member of the Hawks as they were that night—Patrick Hannan as Mickey Jones, who became a successful comedy actor on television; Andrew Claridge as Robbie Robertson, who turned to the movies and solo projects after 1976, leaving the rest to struggle on as an oldies act; Tim Keegan as Richard Manuel, who at forty-two hanged himself after a Band show at the Cheek to Cheek Lounge in Winter Park, Florida, in 1986; and Jake Kyle as Rick Danko, who died of a heart attack in 1999, at fifty-six ("There is no Garth Hudson replica on this recording," read the liner notes)—has the song in the air, and Hitchcock, who made his name in the late 1970s with the Soft Boys, a punk-psychedelic group of no special distinction, sounds as if he's found himself. They understand that to make the song happen you have to make the chorus happen, and they do it by making a cacophony at its heart, a tangle of harmonica, trebly guitar, bass notes, hammering drums, the whole piece swirling. For a word it could be Johnny Rotten singing, then Joe Strummer. Together the group finds the defiance in the song, the absolute victory over an imaginary audience, the audience contained in the song, implied by its story, far more than the audience from the historical event that is being at least formally reenacted. It's a victory over anyone who disbelieves in the song—or that Hitchcock and the rest can play it.

This is what Dylan found that night in San Francisco, when, again, he sang the song for the first time. The gospel chorus of Clydie King and Regina Harris seize the song as their own; Dylan sings as if the song no longer belongs to anyone. It is a long moment of ecstasy. You see a great ship plowing the waves, and on its deck a man waving his arms in the air.

Nothing as singular as "Like a Rolling Stone" ever influences anything else in its medium as form or content—its only influence is in the line that it draws. Richard Harris's hilariously lugubrious "MacArthur Park"—with the immortal lines about a cake melting in the rain, "I don't think that I can take it/ Because it took so long to bake it"—was a version of "Like a Rolling Stone" in 1968; so, with Dylan himself stepping out of the crowd of Stevie Wonder, Cyndi Lauper, Bruce Springsteen, Ray Charles, and many more to perpetrate a Dylan parody that would have humiliated a karaoke singer, was USA for Africa's "We Are the World" in 1985, and so was the Temptations' seven-minute "Papa Was a Rollin' Stone" in 1972—for the way it turned Dylan's metaphor inside out. With its nightmare strings and its relentlessly cold, mocking blues guitar, this was the story of a liar and a cheat: a wastrel with barbeque sauce smeared all over his phony preacher's collar, a man who left nothing behind but wreckage and despair. In its own mode, Led Zeppelin's 1971 "Stairway to

Heaven" was a leap for the territory "Like a Rolling Stone"
had mapped out, both in the grandeur of its sound and in its
call for an escape from the Kingdom of Mammon in its
words—an escape into a daydream of Druidic forests while
riding the escalator up to the lingerie floor of Harrod's. No
one saw the line drawn by "Like a Rolling Stone" more
clearly, or took up its challenge more gleefully—to the point
of enlisting Al Kooper to play organ, piano, and French horn,
actress Nanette Newman and singers Doris Troy and Madelaine Bell to lift Mick Jagger's voice off the ground, and the
London Bach Choir to hover over them all like an army of
female saints—than the Rolling Stones did in 1969, with
"You Can't Always Get What You Want," the *fin des années soix-
antes* epic that closed *Let It Bleed*, along with *Highway 61 Revisited* the best rock 'n' roll album ever made. But all of these
songs, masterpieces or embarrassments, were productions;
"Like a Rolling Stone" was a runaway train. Except perhaps in
Jimi Hendrix's 1968 "Voodoo Chile," which was also a version of Muddy Waters's "Rollin' Stone," the sense of real time,
of an event taking place as you listen, of history accumulat-
ing between notes and words as they are played and sung,
was not present at all. That was elsewhere.

Ten years after he released "Like a Rolling Stone," Bob
Dylan, having been carried through the decade by his own
legend, an oddly crepuscular figure who many believed still
carried within himself the secrets of an epoch when Desolation Row was just across the street, emerged from the miasma

of hit albums that people forgot almost as soon as they'd played them. It didn't matter if it was *Self Portrait* and *New Morning* in 1970, both top ten, the number one *Planet Waves* in 1974, or the top-ten *Before the Flood*, a live album from Dylan's 1974 comeback tour with the Band. Go back to this music now, and aside from a stray mystery or a finger pointing in your face—"Sign on the Window" from *New Morning*, "Going, Going, Gone" on *Planet Waves*, "Highway 61 Revisited" from *Before the Flood*—what it says is that a career continued. Why? Why not? What for? Don't ask. That was why *Blood on the Tracks* was a shock.

It was early 1975. For the first time in the history of the republic, a president had resigned; a man for whom not a single person had voted had taken his place. A war that had begun before the name Bob Dylan had been uttered in public had finally been lost; in disgrace, returning soldiers tried to blend in with ordinary men and women, and in an even deeper disgrace, ordinary men and women tried to blend in with themselves. As the country went about its business in a haze of meaninglessness, Dylan, it seemed, was ready to start over, not as a private individual with money to make and children to raise but as a legendary figure of many parts, cool and reflective, drunk and mad, a pathfinder, someone who had been from one end of the land to the other and returned to tell the tale. *Blood on the Tracks* was a spare, unassuming chronicle of a drifter struggling to hold a life together in a country where no one wants him anywhere but gone. The songs were presented without authority, as if the singer had to earn his chance to speak. There were love songs and lost-love songs; there was a Western-cum-detective story so cinematic it's a wonder it remains unfilmed. There were undertones of a mythic story, outside of any place and time ("In a little hilltop village, they gambled for my clothes"— that calls up Richard the Lion-Hearted traveling back from the Crusades to England in disguise as readily as it does a prospector in the Black Hills); nevertheless the sense of an ongoing story, a history taking in the characters in Dylan's past songs and all those who had followed their adventures, was inescapable.

In two long numbers, the five-minute-forty-second "Tangled Up in Blue" and the seven-minute-forty-five-second "Idiot Wind," Dylan rewrote the story of the previous ten years as if the drama in "Like a Rolling Stone" had actually happened. People had set out to live as if no one knew them, as if they had forgotten the names of the streets on which they grew up and even those of the parents who gave them everything or kicked them out. People turned their backs on the past; they told themselves that anything was possible. They took new names, made their way through the country as if in disguise, and as they did so they discovered that they were no longer at home there, that nothing looked the same, that when they walked down streets named Elm or Broadway they could not see their faces in the shop windows as they passed.

In "Tangled Up in Blue," freedom has come down to a series of odd jobs in places you might not have heard of until you woke up in them. The way the singer comes down on "Delacroix" is almost the whole story, the sound of the word enough to make him dig in, dig down. He finds a voice: a jaunty, I'm-from-Missouri tone that can explode into passion and surprise at any time. With a jocular beat putting a spring in his step, he crisscrosses the country, from east to west, north to south—but not the country that makes the news. In that country, people build fortunes and buildings; in the singer's country they work as short-order cooks, fishermen, topless dancers. One-time revolutionaries turn into heroin dealers. Faces rot; eyes go blank; some dress in silk, some sleep in rags on the street, but no one has anything left to say. Still, the singer grins as he leaves, daring time to declare the story over, daring you to follow him as he slams his car door and pulls onto U.S. Highway 61, curious to see if it can take him anywhere it hasn't taken him before.

For all of the miles on his tires, the man singing in "Tangled Up in Blue" is unscarred, unafraid, unfinished, and absolutely sane. Peace of mind is his birthright; the ground beneath his feet is down to earth. But there is no ground beneath the feet of the man singing in "Idiot Wind." As if it were the Hudson River Valley in the eighteenth century and the singer was at once Ichabod Crane and the Headless Horseman chasing him, in the same body, in the same moment, he travels in the air. He lights in Leadville, Col-

orado, in 1890, stalks into a bar, and demands a drink. "They
say I shot a man named Gray, and took his wife to Italy," the
man says to the other customers, speechifying as if he's running for office. "She inherited a million bucks, and when she
died it came to me. I can't help it—if I'm *lucky*." But nobody's
buying, and the bartender says the singer has to pay like anybody else; he shoots the glass out of the bartender's hand and
storms out the door. He wears a rounder's duster, handling
his Winchester like a six-shooter; he wears a New England
preacher's black cloak and carries a knife in a scabbard.

He has nowhere to go and the only story he can tell is
made of curses; all he wants out of life is revenge. The laughing bluster of the man in the bar, trying to cadge a drink out of
his tall tale about the fortune that got away, turns into slit-eyed
hate when he thinks about the woman who got away, or the
self that disappeared; when the singer says, "One day you'll be
in the ditch, flies buzzing around your eyes," you want to
cover your own. There was rage and fear in "Like a Rolling
Stone," finally left behind by the sheer exhilaration of the
adventure the song promised; now there is no promise and
rage and fear are the only currency the singer trusts. But as a
wish to kill the past by murdering whoever wears its face, an
old lover, an old friend, yourself, fragments of the old exhilaration are still there. The storm in "Like a Rolling Stone," the
storm that clears the ground of the familiar and reveals a thousand roads is now a storm of pure destruction, but the lust that
carries the singer toward the storm is the same.

Mapping the social landscape that opened up out of "Like a Rolling Stone," "Tangled Up in Blue" is shapely, a pica-resque with a cute tagline for every verse, our hero pulling out his trusty harmonica, "headin' for another joint"—and in the end the landscape disappears like smoke, the song leav-ing the listener no sense that he or she has been anywhere at all. "Idiot Wind" is all chaos; the emotional depth "Tangled Up in Blue" skips over is very nearly all it has. There is too much happening, too much violence, too much hate, too much fear; as the people in the song tear by you barely catch their shouts. The song is sprawling, ragged, running on empty—but as with the hard, naked organ sound, the story the song tells has been running on empty for years. "Idiot Wind" has no ending, no beginning; it is a single damn that will last for the rest of the singer's life. Finally the two songs are no more than pieces torn from a greater body, echoes of a song that can seem to swallow up whatever presumes to speak its language.

There are songs that truly take place in the country "Like a Rolling Stone" opens up—that follow the trail left by the way of life the song calls for, that it demands, the cutting of all ties, the refusal of all comforts, even your own name. One is Dylan's "Highlands," from 1997, a song much longer than "Like a Rolling Stone"; the other is the Pet Shop Boys' 1993 version of the Village People's 1979 "Go West."

The Village People were pure kitsch. They performed as a catalogue of gay fetishes, with the singers costumed as policeman, construction worker, cowboy, biker, GI, and Indian chief. For a few months they were huge—a gross parody of every homophobic fantasy about homosexuals having a good time, which is to say a spectacle of gay culture even a homophobe could love. More than a quarter century after it was a top ten hit crowds in ballparks shout out the chorus of "Y.M.C.A.," the group's biggest hit, as if it were no more threatening than "Take Me Out to the Ball Game." In 1979, as with the Summer of Love in 1967, people who never felt at home in their own home towns were streaming to the wooden houses and cramped streets of San Francisco's Castro District, the gay neighborhood with its own unofficial gay mayor, Supervisor Harvey Milk. It didn't matter that, along with Mayor George Moscone, Milk had been shot to death by a homophobic fellow supervisor the year before "Go West" hit the charts; this was pop, which made its own time. "Go West" was Scott McKenzie's "San Francisco (Be Sure to Wear Flowers in Your Hair)" twelve years later, and just as cheesy; as history repeating itself, both were versions of "Sweet Betsy from Pike," which the forty-niners sang all the way to San Francisco more than a century before either of them. In 1979 no one had heard of AIDS.

The Pet Shop Boys were as London as fog and gas lights. Neil Tennant sang, synthesizer player Chris Lowe was the band, and from the mid–1980s they fashioned a portrait of modern city life, where the people in their songs could be gay or straight, young or old, questing or waiting. The songs—the unbearably lovely "Rent," a tune about a kept boy that any number of women found themselves singing under their breath as they said yes to the men who paid for their drinks and their dinners; the reserved but blissful "I Wouldn't Normally Do this Kind of Thing"; the glorious "What Have I Done to Deserve This?" with Dusty Springfield; their ethereal cover of the Elvis heartbreaker "Always on My Mind"— were subtle, nuances within nuances, sometimes so delicate it seemed as if one wrong inflection might crack a tune in half. "Go West" was not delicate, and by the time the Pet Shop Boys took it up it had already broken. Even more than Greenwich Village, the place that impresario Jacques Morali, who died of AIDS in 1991, named the Village People for, in 1993 the Castro was a haunted house, a neighborhood of funerals and walking dead. As a friend put it the year before he died, it was a place where people waited "for their number to come up."

This was the voice the Pet Shop Boys put into "Go West" in 1993. There was the sound of seagulls calling, waves crashing on San Francisco's Ocean Beach, and then a sixteen-voice male choir chanting like the Red Army Chorus, loud and manly and indomitable. In his thin, nearly apologetic voice, the voice of someone who has never completely believed that he deserves to be happy, Neil Tennant followed. "TOGETHER," announced the choir. "We will go our way," Tennant answered.

TOGETHER we will fly so high
TOGETHER tell all our friends good-bye
TOGETHER we will start life new
TOGETHER this is what we'll do

"GO WEST," sang the chorus. "This is our destiny," Tennant sang, the enormous idea small but undeniable in his mouth. Flags unfurled; the wind blew them straight. The sound was like the sun, the disco beat stirring, the drum machine a twentieth-century Yankee Doodle. The song gathered the whole of the American story to itself, claimed it as its own, and said that it would never end. "There where the air is free," sang Tennant, "we'll be"—"WE'LL BE," answered the choir—"what we want to be." "AHHH AHHH *AHHHH*," sang the chorus, rising on its own air. "Now," Tennant sang, following in the footsteps of millions, from Sir Walter Raleigh to Daniel Boone, Calamity Jane to Long Island–born Harvey Milk himself, "if we make our stand, we'll find"— "WE'LL FIND"—"our promised land."

And then the song took off, over mountains, through valleys, across rivers, across oceans, each line more expansive, more triumphant, heroic, and modest than the last, for the singers were claiming no more than what anyone else could take as a birthright. As the choir thundered again and again, with Tennant oddly taking its place and the choir his—

Go west IN THE OPEN AIR
Go west BABY YOU AND ME
Go west THIS IS OUR DESTINY!

—you rose to the story as you listened, eager to join it, even
if, then, if not before, you realized that the massed voice of
the choir stood for all the voices of the dead, and Tennant,
thirty-nine in 1993, was the voice of an adventure that had
come to an end before he was ready to take part. As you listen, you hear history tearing the song to pieces—but the
song will not surrender its body. At five minutes it seems to
go on forever, and you want it to. You can't play it once.

Dylan's "Highlands," as it closed *Time Out of Mind* in
1997—the album was a Western, really, made of ghost towns
and bad weather, as complete and uncompromised a piece of
American art as Philip Roth's 1997–2000 trilogy of *American
Pastoral*, *I Married a Communist*, and *The Human Stain*—was sixteen minutes long. Depending on your mood, or Dylan's performance—on stage, this first-person tale of a man in his
fifties or sixties leaving his house and going for a walk, speaking only to a waitress, watching the people around him, feeling used up, dead, forgotten by whoever might remember
him and cursed by the fact that he can still remember himself, could be sly, withdrawn, teasing, an endless joke or a
digressive suicide note—"Highlands" can feel as if it could fill
up the whole day, as the adventures the man recounts have

filled his, or begin and end in the time it takes to walk around the block. The singer is in no hurry. He looks at the people passing him by; they don't look at him. He wonders if he ever belonged anywhere; he doesn't care if he did or not. No one kicks him into the gutter; if anyone did, he'd get up and brush himself off. Vehemence rises out of him like smoke; he lets it go into the air, and watches as it does.

Here, in a song that begins with a poem by Robert Burns, itself a recasting of a Scots folk song, the line that "Like a Rolling Stone" drew can no longer be seen. It's there, the singer may even know precisely where it is, but no one else does, and no one else wants to know. The country that song opened up was named Highway 61 in 1965; now it is called the Highlands. To find yourself riding out of "Like a Rolling Stone" onto Highway 61 was to feel as the song said you should feel, without a home; "Highlands" is about a mythical place where you will feel absolutely at home, and it tells the tale "Like a Rolling Stone" couldn't tell, and that *Highway 61 Revisited* hid in its corners: you can be at home only in your idea of where you are from, whether that idea is ruled by the hypocrisies described in "With God on Our Side" or the lingering sense that, perhaps, God is. So Dylan's highlands, like his fellow Minnesotan F. Scott Fitzgerald's old American republic, recede as they are pursued, and thus they stay in the air as an inviolable image of the good—an image, the singer says as he walks through a city where he can barely bring himself to talk and where almost no one hears him if he does, that he can bring down into his heart if he must. If he does that, though, it will no longer hang in the air, as a picture of the world as it ought to be, so he leaves it there.

The unmapped country prophesied in "Like a Rolling Stone" is still there too, hanging in the air as a territory of danger and flight, abandonment and discovery, truth and lie, but as "Highlands" plays, there is the sense that no one has been there for years. The singer has long since traversed that country; he knows his way around. He wouldn't mind company, but he can do without it. Every once in a while he hears his old song on the radio, and the country is new again; that will have to do.

Epilogue

15 June 1965, Studio A, Columbia Records, New York City

With Michael Bloomfield, guitar, Frank Owens, organ, Joe Macho, Jr., bass, Bobby Gregg, drums, and Al Gorgoni, guitar, Bob Dylan has recorded nine takes of "Phantom Engineer" and six takes of "Sitting on a Barbed Wire Fence."

Take 1—1.11

"Let's roll, Larry—there's no—ah, I better slate it," Tom Wilson says. "Uh, CO 86446. 'Like a *Rolling* Stone'—*one*." Dylan tests a note on harmonica. Bloomfield counts off: "One two, one two three"—and Bobby Gregg hits the snare drum, lightly. They enter the song very slowly, all covered by a

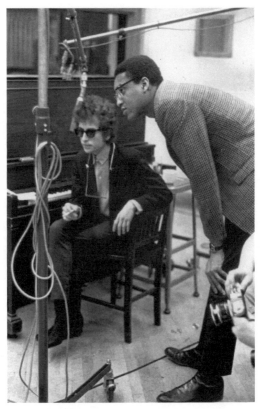

With Tom Wilson

bleating harmonica, which drifts into a long lament—close to the solos Dylan would play in 1966 on "Sad-Eyed Lady of the Lowlands" on *Blonde on Blonde*—as the band drops into the theme.

Dylan: "It got lost, man. It didn't get lost?" Sounding eager, upbeat: "It did get lost. Try it again." He blows his harmonica. Bloomfield begins to run down the song: "Two bars and an E bar B flat minor—"

Take 2 a–c—3.01

"—there's two bars . . . Hey, Bob, is that like"—then Dylan, with his characteristic percussive style, is demonstrating on the piano, banging a stately, somewhat martial theme as Bloomfield comes in with high notes, working out the structure of the song, trying to lift it up. Bloomfield: "OK, it's two bars of E flat minor, one bar E flat minor suspended, E flat minor seven on the next one, four bars in the"—and he's drowned out by a big, melodramatic Hammond sound from Owens, like the accompaniment to a 1940s radio play: "Who knows what evil lurks in the hearts of men? The Shadow knows!" "Hey," Bloomfield says. "Hold it, fellas: the four bars before C, E flat minor suspended fourth, E flat minor seven, then, one bar of A flat suspension, and then A flat . . . alright? So it should sound like"—and the theme is banged out again. Dylan comes in with a wavering harmonica; Bloomfield follows. "Four bars, before C, is this"—there's the piano, then

the organ, terribly churchy, all wrong. Bloomfield is more
businesslike: "E flat minor suspended fourth—E flat minor
without the seventh, E flat minor suspended," and the group
continues to work out the theme on piano, organ, guitar. "A
flat suspended—no, you got something else in there . . . that's
not it, that's not right." Bloomfield plays a rolling chord.
"That's right . . . So what are C—letter B now has one two
three four, five six seven eight—twelve bars, and then a B.
Eight bars in A, twelve bars in B, ten bars in C—"

"That's right," Dylan says, as if it's not news to him.
Bloomfield laughs, as if to say it might have been easier if
Dylan had been willing to explain this in the first place.
Dylan: "Slowly, now, a little bit slower and softer." Bloom-
field: "Rolling?" Another voice: "80646, or whatever the heck
it is." Wilson: "We were rolling all the time." Bloomfield:
"One two three, two—" The piano and harmonica play: "Too
fast," someone says. "Yeah, OK," Dylan says.

Take 3—1.46

Bloomfield, in a loud, commanding voice: "One two three,
two two"—and there's a big sound, again a very mournful
harmonica. With many sour notes, Bloomfield begins to find
a tune. The organ wrecks whatever is happening; it's over-
broad, and playing in an aggressive, destructively simplistic
manner. Then Bloomfield almost locks into the theme.

"What are you doing?" someone says. There is confusion.

A lot of people are talking at once. "This time," Bloomfield says, the kindergarten teacher growing impatient, because school was over twenty minutes ago and no one has come to pick up their kids, "you only played six bars of C." "I want to hear it through the system speakers," Dylan says. "I'll sing the words." In the background: "That part doesn't fit, the building part doesn't—" "Hey," Bloomfield says, "you know what, if I play it it'd be a lot easier, man, and there'll be just one of us, instead of the changes, because otherwise we're all gonna—" Dylan, impatient in turn: "OK, let's go—no," he says to Bloomfield, "he KNOWS IT, man, he knows it." "Well, I keep hearing, suspension," Bloomfield says. Dylan clears his throat twice, as if to shut him up. He hits a note on his harmonica. "Go ahead," he says. "Four," says Wilson.

Take 4—2.20

Bloomfield: "One two three, two two—" Dylan goes immediately into the first verse. His voice is one drawn-out *ribbit*. The piano bangs, and Dylan adds a squeaking harmonica. A bass appears and drops out. The organ squeaks, but the singing squeaks the most. Dylan reaches the end of the verse, and hangs onto the last word: "Your next meeeaaalll . . ." He reaches the chorus.

This is the take that appeared on Dylan's *the bootleg series, volumes 1–3 [rare and unreleased]*, in 1991. There it sounds pitiful, but in James Marsh's film *Highway 61 Revisited*, where it is used

to orchestrate footage signifying Dylan's arrival in New York,
it sheds its skin and emerges as a folk song, a field recording;
it could be the scratchy wire recording behind Ben Shahn's
1935 Farm Security Administration photo *Doped Singer, 'Love
oh, love, oh keerless love,' Scotts Run, West Virginia*—except that in
Shahn's portrait, the doped singer, sitting in a clearing in a
town that was known to the FSA crew as the poorest place in
the United States, and thus a gold mine, is movie-star handsome. Maybe he's a plant? But as Marsh tracks a car crossing a
bridge into nighttime Manhattan, the feeling is that Dylan's
sound in this fragment is from the deepest backwoods—and
also a cry of anguish with nobody listening but the song
itself, a stab in the dark, a hand grasping the door jamb: *Don't
shut it in my face!*

Beginning with a terribly clunky "You used to make fun
about"—something no one would ever say—on the way to
"Everybody that was hanging out," Dylan jumps the words:
the *"Now"* for "Now you don't" is soulful, suffused with sor-
row. "How does it feel? How does it feel? To be out on your
own—*so alone*," he says, the last two words wistful, regretful:
It didn't have to be this way. "Like a rolling stone." There is a harmonica solo.

"The voice is gone, man," Dylan says. "You want to try it
again? You want to try it again?" Bloomfield: "That's a vamp
until ready. It's a one-four-to-five, like I said. And then we'll
keep doin' that, until he comes back on letter A." "What
about that part, Bob," someone says, "that holding-out part?"

"Oh, yeah!" Dylan says, as if he just woke up for the third time in the last twenty seconds. "That's, that's after I say *rolling* stone.' And we're back up to speed then—and when the next verse comes in, it just hangs on it, see, the harp will just play—"

Bloomfield hits a count of the theme, harshly. Dylan: "You want to try it? One verse?" Bloomfield: "You're not going to hang this one this time—" Dylan: "OK, play it just a little faster—" Bloomfield: "Softly, just a little faster." Dylan: "Just a little bit." Bloomfield: "Are we rolling?" "Yeah, we're continually rolling," Wilson says. Bloomfield plays pretty notes, shaping the theme—and for the first time you hear the hint of a song, of something extraordinary.

Take 4 a—.39

Bloomfield finds a fairy tale sound. A second guitar is tuned high. The harmonica comes in. Bloomfield: "You're not all playing the suspension at the same place." Dylan: "You want to try it?"

Take 5 a–b—3.37

Wilson: "OK, rolling five." Bloomfield counts off: "Uh-one"— he goes into handclaps—"uh-one, uh-one-two-three-four." There are very hesitant drums, playing a clickety-clack beat. "Once upon," Dylan tries to begin: "No, go ahead. I just played the introduction, man, just those two things." "Is that too fast?" "No, that's fine." Bloomfield claps again: "One two three two, three two three four."

They start again with the harmonica introduction, with the words unsteady. But as Dylan nears the end of the first verse his voice fills out, and you can hear his wish for the chorus. Nothing is rushed, but there is pressure building. Dylan reaches the chorus and drives it hard; it draws him in. At this point, "How does it feel?" is very nearly the whole song. "Well!" Dylan says with satisfaction, precisely in time, swinging the word. "Was that any good, or what?" someone asks. Dylan is enthusiastic: "Yeah, yeah."

"Well, that's the format," Bloomfield says. "And when he does the second verse, he stays on that A suspended"—there's a demonstration on piano—"for the second time. I don't know what happens after *that*—you're playing the suspended, right?" There is a lighter, higher theme on the piano. "That's how it's supposed to be," someone says. Bloomfield plays the theme with confidence. There is a lot of cross-talk. "We done for the day?" someone asks.

"Uh, Frank," someone says, "would you give me a form, please?" "Hey, can we hear anything we did today, man?" Dylan asks, realizing they are getting nowhere. "Yeah," Wilson says. Dylan: "Take of, uh, 'Phantom Engineer'?" "Yeah, OK," Wilson says. "Uh, Larry? Let me have, uh, 'Phantom Engineer,' this'll be, take—" The tape is turned off and soon enough everyone is gone.

16 June 1965

Al Kooper is at the organ; Paul Griffin is at the piano; Bruce
Langhorne is playing tambourine. Al Gorgoni and Frank
Owens are not present.

Rehearsal take 1—1.53

Dylan leads the group into the song with a strong, strummed
theme on his electric rhythm guitar. Paul Griffin has a loose,
free bounce on the piano; Kooper immediately has a high, clear
tone. Dylan stops it: "Hey, man, you know, I can't, I mean, I'm
just me, you know. I can't, really, man, *I'm just playing the song*. I
know—I don't want to scream it, that's all I know—" He takes
up the theme again; Bloomfield and Gregg come in. The feeling
is right all around; a rich ensemble is coming together.

Hoarsely, Dylan starts the second verse—"Never turned
around to see the frowns"—and you can feel Bloomfield finding his groove. "You never understood that it ain't no
good"—and it breaks off, just when it was getting exciting.
From the control booth: "Bob, just you alone, so you can hear
what your guitar sounds like, on this amplifier. Only you,
please, for a minute." Dylan plays the lead-in, again, the
rhythm behind "Once upon a time," a small, twirling dance
around something that is yet to appear, and you begin to
hear how the whole song is structured around those four
words, that idea: how the purpose of the song is to make a

stage for them. "That's enough," says the voice from the booth. "We can play it back for you."

Rehearsal take 2—3.03

"Let's do it, man," Dylan says. "Where's Gregg?" says Wilson. "Let's just do one verse, man"—and Dylan again leads on guitar. The tambourine is the first instrument to come in behind him, then a deep, resonant bass, then Bloomfield's guitar, then the organ. There is a lot of space in the sound; it hasn't cohered, and they are not gathering around the singer. Bloomfield is just fingering; there is no attack.

But with "You used to laugh about," both Bloomfield and Kooper step forward, as if recognizing their place in the song. With Dylan coming down on "... *mmmmeeeaaalll*," Bloomfield begins to press, to take off. The moment is immediately lost, and Dylan all but enters the chorus by himself:

> How does it feel?
> How does it feel?
> To be on your own

—and here groaning, as if each word is a burden—

> With no *direction* home
> Like a *complete* unknown
> Like a rolling *stone*

Dylan tries to bridge the gap into the next verse on his harmonica, but what's left of the sound breaks into parts. They stop. Dylan looks for the theme again on his guitar; he and no one else is finding the melody, the point of view, the structure of the song.

Take 1—3.10

Wilson is very laconic: "OK, Bob, we got everybody here, let's do one, and then I'll play it back to you, you can pick it apart"—and then he sees Kooper at the organ. "What are you doing there?" he says with evident amusement. Kooper breaks out laughing. "Hah," Wilson says. Then he too is laughing: "Oh oh oh-kayyyy, stand by. This is CO 86446, 'Like a Rolling Stone,' uh, remake, take one." "Wait a second, man," someone says. "The organ player hasn't found his headset." "You gotta *watch*, Tom," Dylan says. "Hold tape," Wilson says.

There's a count-off, the snare shot and the kick drum making a single noise—and everything flops as it begins, the piano leading but nobody following. Then immediately Kooper picks up the slack, with a distinctive part, and the others play off of his confidence—or his brazenness. But the vocal is drifting, with Dylan searching for the right emphases: *"You used to!"* Bloomfield begins to find his footing—and you can hear how Kooper holds back as he does so. Dylan bears down: *"Now you don't talk so loud"*—and when he reaches *"mmmeeeaaalll,"* that word now plainly the hinge of the song, the magic word that will open its door, Bloomfield catches the rising spirit that will take the verse into the chorus, that thrilling *spring!* and then an upsurge, an exhalation, after the first "How does it feel":

> When you're on your *own*
> Without a home
> Like a complete unknown

—with Dylan singing that line as if he's completely surprised by it, as if he's never heard it before—

> Like a rolling stone

But the drumming is too strong, too loud, and the beat is too crude—fit for a parade. Gregg is taking too much of the rhythm for himself, damaging any sense of a common sound. Kooper improvises on a chorus, but without focus, and he drifts away, toward a reverie. Dylan breaks it off: "Naw, we gotta work that part out." "You said once," a voice says, "but you did it twice." "I did it," Dylan says, "but I *finished* it once, don't you see?" "No." "Like a rolling *stooooonnnnne*," he says, demonstrating on guitar, hitting the strings hard, the theme echoing. "Hold it out," says the voice, "go to the next verse." "No, no, no," Dylan says, "here's what I *mean*"—and again he sets about showing the others what the song is, how they will get from the verse to the chorus, and then he loses focus.

"Hold tape," Wilson says. "Even if we screw it up," Dylan says, a new command in his voice, "we keep going." "OK," Wilson says.

Take 2—.30

There's a bright introduction, but the piano slips, and after "Once upon a time" everything is confused.

Take 3—.19

They have moved on without a break, and in these few seconds a lot happens. With the count-off—"One two, one two three"—Gregg hits his snare and kick drum hard, a huge sound, the big bang, and it's the first true moment of realizing the song, of setting whatever it is they're doing apart from whatever else they've done. The musicians, especially Bloomfield, Griffin, and Kooper, come in smoothly, as if they know where they're going. There is a strong and single sound; they try to get a purchase on the song, to give it definition, a real beginning so it can reach its end—but they break off before Dylan even begins to sing.

Take 4—6.34

"Four," Wilson says. As it happens, this will be the master take, and the only time the song is found.

"One two, one two three": the bang that sets it off is not quite as big as in the take just before, but it somehow makes more space for itself, pushes the others away for the fraction of a second necessary to mark the act. Gregg, too, has found the song. He has a strategy, creating humps in the verses and then carrying everyone over them.

As big as the drums are, Griffin plays with light hands; you can imagine his keys loosening. At the very start, piano and bass seem the bedrock—but so much is happening, and with such gravity, you cannot as a listener stay in one place. You may have heard this performance thousands of times, but here, as it takes shape, the fact that it does take shape doesn't seem quite real. The false starts have created a sense that there can be no finished version, and even if you know this is where it happens, as with all the takes before it you are waiting for it to stop short.

Bloomfield is playing with finesse, passion, and most of all modesty. He has a sense of what to leave out, of when to play and when not to. He waits for his moments, and then he leaps. And this is the only take where, for him, everything is clear.

There is a moment, just after the first "How does it feel?" when Kooper's organ, Bloomfield's guitar, and Gregg's cymbals come together in a single waterspout, and you can feel the song running under its own power. You wonder: what are the musicians thinking, as this astonishing story, told with such a sensation of daring and jeopardy, unfolds in front of them for the first time?

First steps, first ensemble: from left to right, Bobby Gregg, unidentified guitarist, Al Gorgoni, Michael Bloomfield, Frank Owens, Joe Macho, Jr., Tom Wilson (behind glass), Bob Dylan

Kooper holds down a stop at the fade, long after everyone else has quit playing. "Like wild thing, baby," someone says, beside himself. "That sounds good to me," Wilson says, happiness all over his voice.

Unslated take—1.00

Wilson, confident: "All quiet, go, Bobby." Dylan leads with a harsh guitar sound. "Ready?" he says. "Not ready." "When the red light comes on." Dylan goes back to his guitar: "No good, huh?" "Keep going," someone says. "Play that back, Pete, please," says someone else.

Take 5—.30

"Hold it just a sec," Wilson says. "OK. Rolling five." Griffin kicks the song off very fast; Dylan stops him. "That's not it— how do we do it?" "That's not how you do it," someone says. "Well," Dylan says, "how do we do it, man, how do we start it out?" He goes back to the guitar and plays the theme slowly.

Take 6 a–b—2.06

"Six roll," Wilson says, but the take cuts off as soon as the stick hits the snare. "Hold," Wilson says. "Hold." Dylan fingers his guitar, while Bruce Langhorne tries to make a beat on tambourine. Wilson: "You ready, Pete?" "Wait a second,"

Dylan says. "Play one verse, do one verse first, without recording." "OK, rolling six," Wilson says.

"*Ah, no,*" Dylan says with disgust, as if this is the stupidest thing he's ever heard. "Don't roll *six*." He begins the song on guitar. "We're gonna have to do one verse." They go back in. This time there is no snare; the piano keys the fanfare. Dylan begins to sing, but the beat is slipping. The drum beats stand apart from each other, and the whole sound begins to separate into its elements. Bloomfield steps up, with a luminous sound. The singing is fractured, fading, as if Dylan has lost interest, but then he dives for the chorus—and loses it. "Oh, let's cut it . . . it's six minutes long, man," he says, as if someone hasn't gotten the joke. "Only you with the guitar, man," Wilson says.

Take 6 c—.36

"Rolling six," Wilson says. Again Dylan's guitar is harsh; the drums clatter. Dylan stops after "dime." "Take it again, let's take it again," he says. "Is my guitar too loud?"

Take 8 (there is no seven)—4.28

"Stand by, rolling eight," Wilson says. "Doesn't feel good?" says a voice from the booth. "Yeah, it feels alright now," Dylan says. There's a count: "One two—four five seven," and then the snare. Dylan leads on harmonica, the bass is

strong—and the drums have turned martial and busy, under-
mining the song from the start. It's a mess, but it's alive, scat-
tershot, everyone reaching in a different direction. The more
oppressively Gregg plays, Griffin plays more foolishly.
"WHOOAA—you've gone to the finest schools," Dylan
shouts, riding the bucking line. The second verse is crack-
ling, Dylan singing like William and Versey Smith chanting
their version of "The Titanic" on the street in Chicago in
1927 and everyone agreeing that, yes, it sure was sad when
that great ship went down, but everyone grinning, too,
because it was such a great ship, and it went *down*, and they
didn't. "Whooaa—you never turned around, to watch"—
Dylan is flying solo. His rhythm guitar is pushing; Bloomfield
is all but silent. Then Bloomfield picks up a theme from the
piano—he has lost his own hold on the song. *Budda bump,
budda bump*, say the drums, and by now that's all they say. The
take breaks off two words into the last verse. "My guitar's too
loud?"

Take 9—.20

There's a count, a few notes—Wilson whistles it dead.

Take 10—.24

Wilson, sounding weary: "Ten." Again a count, notes, whistle.
"There's something wrong," he says. "Timewise."

Take 11—6.02

Dylan, again with disgust: "Say something's wrong *time*—"
"Eleven," Wilson says.

As the song starts, Dylan already seems tired of it, and the first line is sing-songy. Everything out of his mouth is forced, each word emptying itself of emotion as it passes. Bloomfield is there only for the lead-ins to the choruses; Kooper presses. Dylan's singing gains force, but the timing is still off, and the drummer is still dropping dead weight. Dylan sings more stridently; he's more effective. But there is no whole—there is barely a song. So much is missing you can think that if everything hadn't come together seven takes back, they could reach forever and miss by more every time.

They're into the fourth verse, for only the second time, and Griffin is playing like Floyd Cramer on "Last Date." There is banging and clashing, but the vocal is beginning to take off. With "You've got no secrets to CONCEAL" the last word shoots up like a balloon with its string cut, tracing a dizzying path in the sky. "Awwwwww," Dylan lets go after the last chorus, carried away, ignoring his harmonica. "Awwwwww—" "I'm afraid I screwed up," he says. The entire take was a screwup, but there were moments only chaos could bring.

Take 12—.29

"Stand by," Wilson says. "OK, we're rollin' for take twelve."
Kooper plays an introduction; Wilson whistles for a stop.

Take 13—1.49

"Hey, Al, lay off on that intro thing there. Thirteen."

Kooper now plays very schematically, as if solving a problem in arithmetic, and it doesn't work—and then on a chorus he goes wild. There is a strange, mysterious underwater sound from the piano. After a verse and a chorus they stop. "Why can't we get that *right*, man," Dylan says, swinging the words more effectively than he was able to do with anything in the actual take. "OK," he says wearily. "Try it again."

Take 14—.22

"Fourteen," Wilson says. The drums are off the beat; Dylan blows the first line.

Take 15—3.18

"Fifteen," Wilson says. Kooper tries out a few lines—in an ice-skating rink. Gregg has lost the song entirely; everything he plays is decoration, but he is decorating something that isn't there. Dylan's voice is full but his singing has no focus. He rushes the chorus, even as Griffin and Bloomfield lock into the cadence the song wants. They get the chorus. The organ gets bigger with every line. And, in a way that pushes him forward, scrambling his timing but allowing him to barrel through anything in his way, his words dissolving and dis-

tant spirits handing them back deformed, now Dylan is
singing off of Gregg's martial beat.

> You say you never
> Compromise
> With the mystery tramp
> Now don't you realize
> He's not selling
> Any alibis
> As you stare into the vacuum of his eyes
> And say unto him

"Unto him"? Where are we, in the Bible?

> Do you
> Want to make
> A DEAL

And then "DEAL," like "CONCEAL" in take eleven,
shoots up, out of the room, out of the building, with a tail of
smoke, and Dylan's head seems to go with it. After "tricks for
you" they lose the beat, and they stumble out of the song.
That was the end of the session.

"I think it's one of those songs that's pretty timeless," Al
Kooper says. "The other one that comes to mind is 'Good

Vibrations.' When you hear it on the radio, it could have come out yesterday. It's a timeless record—so is 'Heartbreak Hotel.' They're putting out something unique, that has not been done before. And because they were recognized, it's become ageless. Which is great. We hear music that was done by people who died before we had a chance to pick up on it—for instance, Robert Johnson. So you're really glad, when you pass on, that you *know* people are going to hear 'Like a Rolling Stone' and 'Good Vibrations' and 'Heartbreak Hotel,' and Robert Johnson. It's a good feeling."

No matter how timeless "Like a Rolling Stone" might turn out to be, what happened over the two days of recording sessions makes it clear that had circumstances been even slightly different—different people present, a different mood in the studio, different weather in the streets outside, a different headline in the morning paper—the song might never have entered time at all, or interrupted it. "I told all the musicians, you quit playing, you're gone," Bob Johnston says of the sessions that followed. "You quit playing, you're never going to hear that song again. Dylan would start a song—they'd be a third of the way through, and someone says, *Waal, I didn't git that*. The bass stops, or the piano player. Dylan would forget about that song and you'd never hear it again." "Like a Rolling Stone" is a triumph of craft, inspiration, will, and intent; regardless of all those things, it was also an accident. Listening now, you hear most of all how much the song resists the musicians and the singer. Except on a single take, when they went past the song and made their performance into an event that down the years would always begin again from its first bar, they are so far from the song and from each other it's easy enough to imagine Bob Dylan giving up on the song, no doubt taking phrases here and there and putting them into another song somewhere down the line but never bothering with that thing called "Like a Rolling Stone" again. Following the sessions as they happened, it can in moments be easier to imagine that than to believe that the record was actually made—that, circling around the song like hunters surrounding an animal that has escaped them a dozen times, they caught it. That is what makes an event, after all: it can only happen once. Once it has happened, it will seem inevitable. But all the good reasons in the world can't make it happen.

WORKS CITED

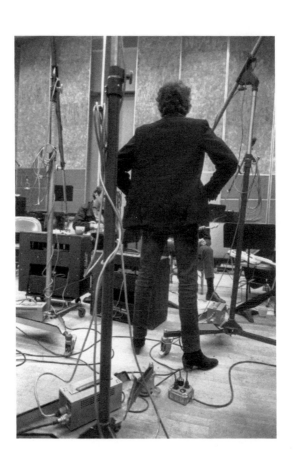

Except when the interviewer or quoting author is mentioned in the text, quotations are noted according to interviewee, in the order in which his or her quotations appear in the text. Films and radio and television programs are noted by title. Recordings by one artist or group are listed by performer; anthologies—recordings by various artists—are listed by title.

Bob Dylan

Referenced collections

the bootleg series, volumes 1–3 [rare & unreleased], 1961–1991 (Columbia, 1991).

The Classic Interviews, 1965–1966 (Chrome Dreams, 2003). Notes by Derek Barker.

McGregor, Craig, ed. *Bob Dylan: A Retrospective*. New York: Morrow, 1972. Reissued as *Bob Dylan: The Early Years—A Retrospective*. New York: Da Capo, 1990.

Recordings

"A Change Is Gonna Come" (Sam Cooke). See *Apollo at 70: A Hot Night in Harlem*. NBC, 19 June 2004.

"Acne." With Ramblin' Jack Elliott. Riverside Church, New York City, broadcast on WRVR-FM, 29 July 1961. Included on Ramblin' Jack Elliott, *The Ballad of Ramblin' Jack—Original Soundtrack* (Vanguard, 2000).

"Blind Willie McTell." Recorded 1983 with Mark Knopfler, guitar. *the bootleg series, volumes 1–3*.

Blonde on Blonde (Columbia, 1966). Includes "Visions of Johanna."

Blood on the Tracks (Columbia, 1975). Includes "Tangled Up in Blue" and "Idiot Wind."

"Blowin' in the Wind." Live performance c. 2000 included on *The Best of Bob Dylan, volume 2* (Columbia, 2000). With the tune picked out on acoustic guitars and the verses crooned, whispered, and overstated ("How many seas must a white dove sail, before she sleeps—sleeps in the sand"), the song is a monster of sentimentality—a sentimentality directed, it seems, more toward the iconic status of the song than the nostalgic status of its various themes. The high, straining passion of every chorus wipes that out, then the next verse wipes out the preceding chorus, until the song is struggling over its own meanings, or its capacity to still generate them, and the musicians, Dylan included, seem mostly interested in how far the melody can take them.

Bob Dylan (Columbia, 1962). Includes "See that My Grave Is Kept Clean" (Blind Lemon Jefferson) and "House of the Risin' Sun" (traditional). See Animals.

Bringing It All Back Home (Columbia, 1965). Includes "It's Alright, Ma (I'm Only Bleeding)" and "Bob Dylan's 115th Dream."

"Buzz-Buzz-Buzz" (recorded by the Hollywood Flames). Dylan's 1958 home recording of the 1957 Los Angeles doo-wop hit, from tapes made with his Hibbing high school friend John Bucklen, can be heard in *Tales of Rock 'N' Roll: Highway 61 Revisited* (James Marsh). See also "Hey Little Richard" in this section.

"Can't Help Falling in Love" (recorded by Elvis Presley). From *Dylan* (Columbia, 1973).

"Confidential" (Sonny Knight). The 1967 version with the Band is included on *A Tree with Roots: The Genuine Basement Tape Remasters* (Wild Wolf bootleg); a superb live performance from Indianapolis, Indiana, 10 November 1991, is on the "Alternates & Retakes" disc of *The Genuine Never Ending Tour: The Covers Collection 1988–2000* (Wild Wolf bootleg).

"Da Do Run Run" (cover of the Crystals' "Da Doo Ron Ron"). Included on *Almost Went to See Elvis* (Cool Daddy bootleg). See Crystals.

"Don't Start Me Talkin'" (Sonny Boy Williamson). The 22 March 1984 performance from *The Late Show with David Letterman* is on *Hard to Find: Volume 2—Extraordinary Performances 1975–95* (Columbus bootleg).

Early 60's Revisited (Trade Mark of Quality bootleg, 1974). Sleeve cartoon by William G. Stout.

The Freewheelin' Bob Dylan (Columbia, 1963). Includes "Masters of War," "Blowin' in the Wind," "A Hard Rain's A-Gonna Fall," and "Talking World War III Blues."

"Handsome Molly" (traditional). Recorded at the Gaslight Cafe, New York City, fall 1962. Included on *Live 1961–2000* (SME, 2001, Japan).

"A Hard Rain's A-Gonna Fall." Recorded at the Gaslight Cafe, New

York City, fall 1962. Included on *Second Gaslight Tape* (Wild Wolf
bootleg).

"Hey Little Richard." Dylan's 1958 home recording of his own compo-
sition, from tapes made with his Hibbing high school friend John
Bucklen, can be heard in *Tales of Rock 'N' Roll: Highway 61 Revisited*
(James Marsh).

"Highlands." From *Time Out of Mind* (Columbia, 1997). A live version of
"Highlands," at just over eleven minutes, kicking off with drunken
howling from the crowd, was included on *The Best of Bob Dylan, volume
2* (Columbia, 2000). Many other versions are available on bootlegs
or on the Internet, and each one I've heard is different from any
other—except that all are as slow as an August day in Minneapolis
and none is anything close to the sixteen minutes of the version from
Time Out of Mind, which makes that performance all the more spectral.

Highway 61 Revisited (Columbia, 1965).

"House of the Risin' Sun" (traditional). Tom Wilson's overdubbed 1965
production of the version released in 1962 on *Bob Dylan* was
included on *Highway 61 Interactive* (Columbia CD-ROM, 1995),
and has since turned up on various bootlegs. An anticipation of
soon-to-be conventional 1965-style Los Angeles folk rock—light
drums, light electric guitar—it's less rock 'n' roll than the jug-band
style versions of "Corrina, Corrina" and "Rocks and Gravel"
recorded for *The Freewheelin' Bob Dylan* three years earlier, not to
mention the version of "That's All Right," Elvis Presley's first single
(see *The Genuine Bootleg Series Take 2*, bootleg), or Dylan's own first
single, the pumped-up bluegrass stomp "Mixed Up Confusion"
(Columbia, 1962; included on *Biograph*, 1985).

"It's Alright, Ma (I'm Only Bleeding)." From *The Bootleg Series, Vol. 6: Live
1964—Concert at Philharmonic Hall* (Columbia, 2004). Notes by Sean
Wilentz. The first performance of the song, released in 1965 on

Bringing It All Back Home. A remarkable contemporary version can be found on *Live at the Santa Cruz Civic Auditorium, March 16 & 15, 2000* (Bootopia bootleg).

"Like a Rolling Stone" (Columbia, 1965). Recorded 16 June 1965. On the occasion of *Rolling Stone* magazine naming "Like a Rolling Stone" the greatest of the "500 Greatest Songs of All Time," Shaun Considine, in 1965 the new-releases coordinator for Columbia Records, published "The Hit We Almost Missed" in the 3 December 2004 issue of the New York *Times.* He related the tale of how the six-minute single had been dumped into the oblivion of "unassigned release" because of objections by the sales and marketing departments—and how, one day, when the company was moving offices, he came upon a discarded demo pressing of the recording, took it home, played it, played it again, and then brought it down to Arthur's, the hottest disco in town, and asked the disc jockey to play it. "Around 11 p.m., after a break, he put it on," Considine wrote. "The effect was seismic. People jumped to their feet and took to the floor, dancing the entire six minutes. Those who were seated stopped talking and began to listen. 'Who is it?' the D.J. yelled at one point, running toward me. 'Bob Dylan!' I shouted back. The name spread through the room, which only encouraged the skeptics to insist that it be played again. Sometime past midnight, as the grooves on the temporary dub began to wear out, the needle began to skip." A disc jockey and a programming director from New York Top 40 stations were present; they called Columbia and demanded their own copies. "Staff meetings were hastily called," Considine wrote. "The release memo came shortly thereafter."
Take 3, 15 June 1965 ("The voice is gone") is included on *the bootleg series volumes 1–3.* Incomplete versions of takes 1, 3, and 5, June 15, and takes 1, 2, 4, 6, 8, 10, and 15, June 16, are secreted within the

various views of Columbia's bare-bones Studio A that can be found on *Highway 61 Interactive* (Columbia CD-ROM, 1995). A highly effective dramatization of the session, based on these takes, was included on the superb BBC Radio 4 documentary, "Soul Music— Programme 5: Like a Rolling Stone," produced by Lindsay Leonard of BBC Birmingham, which aired 27 July 2004. Speakers included Al Kooper, Robbie Robertson, the singer Dana Gillespie, the choreographer Bebe Miller, the critic Michael Gray, C. P. Lee, and myself; see also Paula Radice. On the fullness of the sound in "Like a Rolling Stone," Al Kooper comments: "While doing research for this project, I was sent a CD that chronicled the entire LARS session—in-between yakking as well. I was amazed to note that Dylan's guitar was noticeably in C tuning. I don't think I had ever heard Bob play in C tuning before, and wondered if it was something that Bloomfield had brought to the table—as it is more common in blues than in folk music. The guitar is tuned to a C chord and the low E-string is lowered down to a C. In common open-chord tunings like G or D, both detune the E to a D, so the C is a rarer choice—to the best of my knowledge, first employed by Bukka White in the '30s and '40s. Because the final mix of LARS has Bob's guitar and my organ in exactly the right place, level-wise, it may not be apparent on the average listen, but the C tuning causes a certain frequency range to be filled that would most certainly not be if Bob was in regular tuning. And now back to our regularly scheduled book."

The 25 July 1965 performance at the Newport Folk Festival is included, along with "Maggie's Farm," "Phantom Engineer," "It's All Over Now, Baby Blue," and "Mr. Tambourine Man," on numerous bootlegs, including *Live in Newport 1965* (Document, 1988); footage of the dynamic "Maggie's Farm" performance can be seen in *The History of Rock 'n' Roll: Plugging In*, directed by Susan Steinberg

(Time-Life Video, 1995). A tinny, distant audience recording of the entire Forest Hills concert, from 28 August 1965, which captures crowd action far more fully than stage action, is included on *Dylan: 1965 Revisited* (Great Dane bootleg), a 14-CD set devoted to the revival of Scholasticism. "Like a Rolling Stone" was the finale, as it was at the 3 September 1965 performance at the Hollywood Bowl, captured in its entirety on *We Had Known a Lion* (Vigotone bootleg, 1998), with notes composed of Shirley Poston's 2 October 1965 concert report for KRLA's *The Beat*. A further 1965 performance of the song can be heard on *Long Distance Operator* (Wanted Man bootleg), recorded at the Berkeley Community Theatre on December 4; when Dylan sings the words "mystery tramp" it's with a queer familiarity, as if he's referring to somebody everyone already knows.

The ultimate, post-"Judas!" performance of "Like a Rolling Stone" from Dylan and the Hawks' May 1966 tour of Ireland and the U.K.—from Manchester, on May 17, which is to say about a minute post-"Judas!"—is on *The Bootleg Series Vol. 4: Live 1966—The 'Royal Albert Hall' Concert* (Columbia, 1998, with notes by Tony Glover), so called because the electric half of the concert was long bootlegged as such. The true Royal Albert Hall performance of the song, from May 27, the last night of the tour, with Dylan's introduction of the Hawks, can be found on *The Genuine Bootleg Series Take 2* (bootleg). It is a rendition of violence: Mickey Jones counts down on each measure and Rick Danko thumps above it, as if the song is a boxer's light bag; in the third verse, the force of "Ain't it hard, when you discover that" is frightening. In the following chorus Dylan's voice almost gets away from him, a hawk he can't control, and he comes into the final verse tired, flagging, falling, the song now not four-and-a-half-minutes long but four hours; by the end of the verse he's gone over a cliff, hollering in the air on the way down.

Other striking performances of the number are from Edinburgh, May 20, on *Sings the Body Electric* (Parrot bootleg) and on the 8-CD set *Genuine Live 1966* (Wild Wolf bootleg), and from Liverpool (the concert recording includes two minutes of "Crowd"), on May 14, on *Genuine Live 1966*, which in its elaborate packaging features the Columbia ad for "Like a Rolling Stone": "A 6 MINUTE SINGLE? WHY NOT! when you have 6 minutes of BOB DYLAN." The 1966 Scandinavian-Irish-U.K. performances were filmed by D. A. Pennebaker for *Eat the Document*, directed by Howard Alk and Dylan, made for ABC television but rejected, and, until a series of screenings at the Museum of Television and Radio in New York and Los Angeles in 1998, complete with period TV commercials, only rarely seen since. The songs in *Eat the Document* are cut up and reassembled from several different performances, to extraordinary effect; the theme of the film is the artist versus the crowd, and includes Keith Butler's "He wants shooting" comment ("a North Country fatwa," Bleddyn Butcher called it in "The Butler Did It!" *Uncut Legends #1: Dylan*, 2003, 30) immediately following his "Judas!" shout—a moment noticeably omitted from Andy Kershaw's "The Ghost of Electricity," a radio documentary on the Manchester concert. Pennebaker made his own, unfinished film of the tour, "Something Is Happening," which has never been publicly screened; there is no theme, but the songs are presented as single bodies, most astonishingly with "Like a Rolling Stone," at the end, with Dylan, or the dervish standing behind him, singing through his cupped hands. ("His idea of putting on a show that stunned people, that's what made him happy," Pennebaker said of the tour in 1998.) More detailed comment on Dylan and the Hawks in the U.S. and the U.K. can be found in my *The Old, Weird America: The World of Bob Dylan's Basement Tapes*, New York (Henry Holt, 1997, as *Invisible Republic*): Picador USA, 2000, in the U.K.

titled *Invisible Republic: Bob Dylan's Basement Tapes*, London: Faber & Faber, 1997, and in Germany titled *Basement Blues: Bob Dylan und das alte, unheimliche Amerika*, Hamburg: Rogner & Bernhard, 1998.

There are many post–1966 recordings of the song by Dylan on official albums, including those drawn from the 1974 tour with the Band and the 1995 MTV *Unplugged* show. The most and least memorable versions I've heard, from the Warfield Theatre in San Francisco on 12 November 1980 to the all-star extravaganza on *Late Night with David Letterman* on 6 February 1992 (NBC), have almost certainly been bootlegged—everything else has been.

"Little Maggie." From *Good as I Been to You* (Columbia. 1992).

"Love and Theft" (Columbia, 2001).

"Masters of War." As performed during the first Iraqi-American war on the Grammy Awards telecast, 20 February 1991, with John Jackson and Cesar Diaz, guitars, Tony Garnier, bass, and Ian Wallace, drums, preceded by an introduction by Jack Nicholson and followed by an acceptance speech by Dylan. Included on *You Don't Know Me*, a valuable 4-CD collection of 1962–1992 live performances (Great Dane Bootleg).

The song came back like a lion when in the fall of 2002 President George W. Bush made plain his intent to launch a second Iraq war. On November 11 of that year, at Madison Square Garden in New York City, just after the mid-term congressional elections that Bush had used the specter of war to win, and that boosted his hand, Dylan gathered Garnier on bass fiddle and Charlie Sexton and Larry Campbell on acoustic guitars around him in a circle, as if they were a coven, and the curse of the song was like something dug out of the ground. In May 2003, with the war underway, Scott Amendola and Carla Bozulich of Berkeley put a nine-minute version of the song on www.protest-records.com. There were moments where the storm they made—with Eric Crystal's shredding saxophone solo at its heart—made it difficult to remember what you were listening to. They took the song's rage almost into the realm of abstraction—until the end, when the instrumentation dropped away, and there was nothing left but taps, silences, and a single voice. Then in October 2004, with Bush and John Kerry battling for Minnesota, Mark Treehouse of Minneapolis, recording as Brother Mark and the Dylanger Four, and working with the punk singer Curtiss A. and the hip-hop assemblage Atmosphere, put out a ranting recital of the tune—with Attorney General John Ashcroft, Bush, Vice-President Dick Cheney, and Secretary of Defense Donald Rumsfeld in red, white, and blue on the cover. On November 2, on election night, in Oshkosh, Wisconsin, with the votes cast but the outcome of the election still unknown, Dylan offered the song once more, dead in the middle of a war, just days before the beginning of an offensive that Bush had put off until his return to office was assured. At first Dylan's delivery was clipped, the words at once rushed and stuttered; the backing was light but doomstruck. "You put a gun in my hand," Dylan sang in the voice of an old frontiersman; it sounded like "You put a gun to my head." "Woo, woo!" people chanted in the crowd. An electric guitar came down hard, then shot out into a rough, twisting solo that never really stopped. Deep troughs opened up in Dylan's voice; with Deadheads throwing hippie whoops out of the audience, he could not have been more serious. "I'll stand over your grave 'til I'm sure that you're dead"—there was no sense that the line had ever been sung before. Dylan's voice was shaking at the end; nothing was held back. And none of this, really, matched what happened at Boulder High School in Boulder, Colorado, the very next day.

On November 3, students staged a sit-in in the school library—because, said freshman Sara Bernstein, "Bush will directly effect our generation's future, and we were upset that we didn't have a choice in that." Principal Ron Cabrera refused to have the students removed; the next morning they were still there, along with news trucks. Democratic Congressman Mark Udall came to the school to speak; Democratic U.S. Senator-elect Ken Salazar scheduled a talk as well. And then the stakes were raised. Calling themselves the Taliband, a group of students began rehearsing a version of "Masters of War" for the school talent show scheduled for November 12. Other students, hearing Allyse Wojtanek-Watson singing the last verse of the song—"And I hope that you die/ And your death will come soon"—called a local talk radio station with the news that students had changed the song to call for Bush's assassination. The arrival of the Secret Service made the national news; agents left with a copy of the lyrics. "If you think it has to do with Bush," Wojtanek-Watson said, "that's because you're drawing your own conclusions." "There's nothing in there about killing Bush," band leader Forest Engstrom said. The group changed its name—to Coalition of the Willing. Parents and radio hosts demanded that the students be kept out of the show.

They played. "A punk rendition," Brittany Anas wrote in the *Daily Camera* on November 13. "Still sweaty from performing, Allyse Wojtanek received congratulations from her friends in the lobby at Boulder High School. Perspiration had run Allyse's thick black eyeliner into her bright green eye shadow after she poured her emotions and voice in the lyrics of a song that has erupted into controversy." "'We were misunderstood,' Allyse said after the show ... 'People thought we were like communists, and that was not it at all. We have a peaceful message.'" "We think that the war we are involved in is wrong, and that people need to come to their senses," band member Brian Martens told Anas. "That's what our music is about." "The singer was drowned out by the guitar," Bernstein said. "You could hear 'war' and 'I hope that you die.' The audience cheered really loud—they liked it." Anas ended her story with an open door: "Analise Nelson, a junior at Boulder High, joked that students at her school want fake IDs so they can vote. Analise's band, Down with Rhonda, a group of six students that got together almost a year ago, also romped around on the stage performing at the talent show. 'I think a lot of kids here are passionate—about music, art, democracy. We've got passion.'"

"New Minglewood Blues" (Noah Lewis). A startling 24 June 1996 performance from Differdange, Luxembourg, can be found on *I've Got a Song to Sing: A Compilation of Rare Performances in 1996* (no label bootleg).

"No Money Down" (Chuck Berry). The encore performance on the illiterately credited Dylan bootleg *Where the Corn Grows Tall—Merriville Pavalion, Merriville, Indiana 10/19/81* (Mystic). Larry Keegan's hipster vocal makes Berry's tale of buying a Cadillac feel like a dope deal; the band falls easily into a slow, heavy Chicago blues vamp, with dirty guitar chords hanging in the air here and there; Dylan's garage saxophone pushes the tune from the start, then slides down the lines of the rhythm with ease.

"No More Auction Block" (aka "Many Thousands Gone," traditional). Recorded at the Gaslight Cafe, New York City, fall 1962. *the bootleg series, volumes 1–3.*

"Phantom Engineer." This frantic early version of the *Highway 61 Revisited* number "It Takes a Lot to Laugh, It Takes a Train to Cry" (one take was mistakenly included on some copies of the album) can be found on *Dimestore Medicine* (Joker bootleg), the 3-CD *Church with No Upstairs: Studio Outtakes 1965/1966* (Hanging Dog bootleg), and, from 25 July 1965, on *Live in Newport 1965* (Document bootleg, 1988).

"Positively 4th Street" (Columbia, 1965).

"Seems Like a Freeze-Out." Early versions of "Visions of Johanna," from *Blonde on Blonde*—a loose, bluesy take from 30 November 1965, and a much more stately performance from 21 January 1966, both probably cut with the Hawks (Bobby Gregg replacing Levon Helm)—are collected on various bootlegs, notably *Thin Wild Mercury Music* (Spank) and, with thinner sound, *Church with No Upstairs: Studio Outtakes 1965/1966*. Live solo versions of "Visions of Johanna" are on *Biograph* (Columbia, 1985), 26 May 1966, and *The Bootleg Series Vol. 4: Live 1966—The 'Royal Albert Hall' Concert* (Columbia, 1998).

"Sitting on a Barbed Wire Fence." This early, big-beat, outrageously swinging version of the *Highway 61 Revisited* number "Just Like Tom Thumb's Blues" (there's nothing more rhythmically perfect in Dylan's career than the way he says "Al*right*" at the end of a phrase), recorded just before Dylan's first attempts at "Like a Rolling Stone," can be found on *the bootleg series, volumes 1–3*, with an alternate take on *Church with No Upstairs: Studio Outtakes 1965/1966*.

"Subterranean Homesick Blues" (Columbia, 1965).

Time Out of Mind (Columbia, 1997). An Australian version of the album, widely available in the U.S. and the U.K., adds seven live bootleg-style "field recordings" (i.e., recordings with audience response, if not recorded in the audience), including three numbers from *Time Out of Mind*. *Not Standing in the Doorway with the Dirt Road Blues (Just Yet)* (Wild Wolf bootleg, 1999) collected live versions of nine songs from *Time Out of Mind*, including an inflamed "'Til I Fell in Love with You."

The Times They Are A-Changin' (Columbia, 1963). Includes "The Lonesome Death of Hattie Carroll." William Zantzinger, her killer, went on to live a notorious life as a criminal Maryland landlord, repeatedly sued and even jailed for refusing to maintain houses rented to

African-Americans at inflated prices or collecting rent on properties he did not own, with every news story framing his offenses with the tale Dylan had told years before. "He's a no-account son of a bitch," Zantzinger said of Dylan in the late 1990s. "He's just like a scum of a bag of the earth." Howard Sounes, *Down the Highway: The Life of Bob Dylan*. New York: Grove Press, 2001. 142.

"With God on Our Side." From *The Times They Are A-Changin'* (Columbia, 1963). The version from Dylan's *MTV Unplugged* (Columbia, 1995), which was as much a recasting of Dylan's black-and-white polka dot shirt as any song, was the strongest piece in the set.

Citations

"What happens if they have to cut a song in half." Press conference, San Francisco, 3 December 1965. *The Classic Interviews, 1965–1966*.

"Eight of the Top Ten." Anthony Scaduto, *Bob Dylan*. New York: Grosset and Dunlap, 1971. 175.

"I've never written." See Hentoff. In McGregor, 134.

"I'll bet Tony Bennett." See Hentoff. In McGregor, 135.

"I had never thought" and "Telling someone something." Jules Siegel. "Well, What Have We Here?" *Saturday Evening Post*, 30 July 1966. In McGregor, 158.

"All I know." From Pat Thomas, "Is It Rolling, Bob?" the definitive work on producer Bob Johnston's work with Dylan. Unpublished, 2001. Courtesy Pat Thomas.

"Desolation Row" as Dylan's "America the Beautiful." See Hentoff. In McGregor, 145.

"You can't tell." Press conference, San Francisco, 3 December 1965. *The Classic Interviews, 1965–1966*.

Akers to Zappa

Akers, Garfield. "Cottonfield Blues Part I and Part II" (Vocalion, 1929). Collected on *Son House and the Great Delta Blues Singers: Complete Recorded Works in Chronological Order, 1928–1930* (Document, 1990). In 1962 "Cottonfield Blues" could be found along with House's "My Black Mama" on *Really! The Country Blues* (Origin Jazz Library).

Animals. "House of the Rising Sun" (MGM, 1964). The full-length version, shaped by organist Alan Price, is on *The Best of the Animals* (ABKCO, 1987), which also features "I'm Crying" and the hilarious "Story of Bo Diddley," and on *Retrospective* (ABKCO, 2004), with bottomless sound and later LSD epics. Price, who appears in *Don't Look Back*, said that the Animals' versions of both "House of the Rising Sun" and "Baby Let Me Take You Home" (a rewrite of "Baby Let Me Follow You Down") came from Dylan's first album; Animals' singer Eric Burdon told Joan Baez it came from *her* first album. In any case, the transfer, if that is what it is, of the song from Dylan to the Animals and, in Al Kooper's organ playing, back to Dylan for "Like a Rolling Stone," is folk music as the pop process, or pop music as the folk process, if anything is.

Articolo 31. "Come una Pietra Scalciata." From *Nessuno* (Ricordi/BMG, 1998). See *Masked and Anonymous: Music from the Motion Picture*. Having named their group for the article in the Irish constitution guaranteeing freedom of the press, J. Ax and DJ Jad of Milan recorded *Nessuno* ("Nobody"), their fourth album, in New York. Complete Italian lyrics can be found at www.angolotesti.it/A/testi_canzoni_articolo_31_32/testo_canzone_come_una_pietra_scalciata_1918.html

Baez, Joan. "John Riley," from *Joan Baez* (Vanguard, 1960). A more complete alternate take is included on the 2001 Vanguard reissue.

Belzer, Richard. See Terry Gross.

Bennett, Will. "Railroad Bill" (Vocalion, 1929). On the anthology *The Early Blues Roots of Bob Dylan* (Catfish, 2000).

Berry, Chuck. *The Autobiography*. New York: Crown, 1987. 219.

———"Johnny B. Goode" (Chess, 1958).

Black Labels. "Rainy Day Women #12 & 35." From *Duluth Does Dylan* (Spinout, 2001).

Bloomfield, Michael. "Dylan Goes Electric." In *The Sixties*, ed. Lynda Rosen Obst. New York: Rolling Stone/Random House, 1977. "I was cheering" (150); "I was wearing" (150); "To the folk community" (151); "In penance" (151).

———"Impressions of Bob Dylan." *Hit Parader*, June 1968. "It's such an old story" (26); credited quotations (24, 26). Courtesy B. George and the ARChive of Contemporary Music.

———"Michael Bloomfield: The Rolling Stone Interview" (Jann Wenner). *Rolling Stone*, 6 April 1968. Collected in *The Rolling Stone Interviews*. New York: Pocket Books, 1971. "I play sweet blues" (46, re 1971); "You had to be as good" (56); "I bought a Fender" (63).

———"You can hear this." From an interview with Tom Yates, 13 February 1981. Quoted in Ed Ward, *Michael Bloomfield: The Rise and Fall of an American Guitar Hero*. Port Chester, NY: Cherry Lane Books, 1983. 8–9. See also Paul Butterfield Blues Band.

Bronstein, Marvin. Interview with Bob Dylan (20 February 1966, Montreal). See *The Classic Interviews, 1965–1966*.

Butler, Keith. See "The Ghost of Electricity" and, regarding the entry on "Like a Rolling Stone," *Eat the Document*.

Butterfield Blues Band. See Paul Butterfield Blues Band.

Byrds. "Mr. Tambourine Man" (Columbia, 1965). "'Like a Rolling Stone' virtually went unnoticed by me in 1965," my friend Fritz Schneider wrote in 2004 of Dylan's reception in West Germany. "In those days, Bob Dylan was, for me and my friends (all born in or around 1953), nothing more than the composer of that fantastic new Byrds single 'Mr. Tambourine Man'—and his own version couldn't hold a candle to their version. For us Dylan was just a folkie with no rock 'n' roll credibility whatsoever—a guy, like Donovan or, a bit later, Leonard Cohen, Cat Stevens, or James Taylor, exclusively treasured by our female classmates."

In 1992, at a televised concert at Madison Square Garden marking Dylan's thirtieth anniversary as a recording artist, Roger McGuinn, the founder of the Byrds, looking at once proud and shy, just a bit uncertain, appeared with Tom Petty and the Heartbreakers to sing "Mr. Tambourine Man" one more time. He launched into the song with the same ringing Rickenbacker twelve-string notes and the same fey voice that made it a hit in the first place; then he passed the single verse of the song he'd used with the Byrds and lunged for the next one. He became a different person. Suddenly his voice thickened; he rocked back and forth on his heels. There was a vehemence in his tone he had never had before; on the "and" in "And if you hear vague traces," his voice lifted into the air and the word broke into fragments, which floated down as pieces of some ancient Scots ballad. Before you could register what you were hearing, McGuinn was already making the hard consonants of the next words into weapons, hammering *"skkkkipping reels of rhyme"* like a blacksmith. See Dylan, *The 30th Anniversary Concert Celebration* (Columbia, 1993; Columbia Music Video, 1993).

Cantwell, Robert. *When We Were Good: The Folk Revival*. Cambridge, MA: Harvard University Press, 1996. 1.

Clark, Petula. "Downtown" (Warner Bros., 1964).

Cooke, Sam. "Blowin' in the Wind." From *Sam Cooke at the Copa* (RCA, 1964).

———"A Change Is Gonna Come" (RCA Victor, 1964). Perhaps best heard today on Cooke, *Portrait of a Legend: 1951–1964* (ABKCO, 2003).

———"Geez." Daniel Wolff with S. R. Crain, Clifton White, and G. David Tenenbaum, *You Send Me: The Life and Times of Sam Cooke.* New York: William Morrow, 1995. 291. See also Rod Stewart.

Cortázar, Julio. *Hopscotch* (as *Rayuela*, 1963). New York: Random House, 1966, trans. Gregory Rabassa. The expats in a Paris apartment in the 1950s, 78s following one after the other like bottles: "all those old records, showboats, Storyville nights, where the only really universal music of the century had come from, something that brought people closer together than UNESCO, or airlines, a music which was primitive enough to have gained such universality and good enough to make its own history . . . a music that could be known in Copenhagen as well as Mendoza or Capetown, a music that brings adolescents together, with records under their arms, that gives them names and melodies to use as passwords so they can know each other and become intimate and feel less lonely surrounded by bosses, families, and bitter love affairs, a music that accepts all imaginations and tastes, a collection of instrumental 78's with Freddie Keppard or Bunk Johnson, the reactionary cult of Dixieland, an academic specialization in Bix Beiderbecke, or in the adventures of Thelonious Monk, Horace Silver, or Thad Jones, the vulgarities of Erroll Garner or Art Tatum, repentance and rejection, a preference for small groups, mysterious recordings made with false names and strange titles and labels made up on the spur of the moment, and that whole freemasonry of Saturday nights in a student's room or in some basement café . . . all this from a kind of music that horrifies solid citizens who think that nothing is true unless there are programs and ushers." 69–70.

Costello, Elvis. "What I've Learned" (interview with Tom Junod). *Esquire*, September 2003. 160.

Cropper, Steve. From "Booker T. and the MGs: The Rolling Stone Interview" (Jann Wenner). *Rolling Stone*, 12 October 1968. Collected in *The Rolling Stone Interviews*. New York: Pocket Books, 1971. 156.

Crouch, Stanley. "Come Sunday," in *The Rose & the Briar: Death, Love and Liberty in the American Ballad*, ed. Sean Wilentz and Greil Marcus. New York: W. W. Norton, 2004. 246. See also "When Watts Burned," in *The Sixties*, ed. Lynda Rosen Obst. New York: Rolling Stone/Random House, 1977.

Crowell, Rodney. "The Times They Are A-Changin': A Radio Symposium on Bob Dylan and His Times," WFUV-FM, New York City, 5 March 2004.

Crystals. "Da Doo Ron Ron" (Philles, 1963).

Curtis, Lucious. "High Lonesome Hill." Recorded 19 October 1940 in Natchez, Mississippi, by Alan Lomax. Collected on *Mississippi Blues: Library of Congress Recordings, 1940–1942* (Travelin' Man, 1973, 1979).

Debord, Guy. "Le déclin et la chute de l'économie spectaculaire-marchande." Dated December 1965, this shocking analysis of the Watts riots ("Looting is the *natural* response to the society of abundance ... The flames of Watts *consummated* the system of consumption") was written in Paris in French, but first published in English as a piece of action literature under the name of the Situationist International, a small group of mostly European writers and artists. It was published anonymously in *Internationale situationniste* 10 (Paris, March 1966), and as "The Decline and Fall of the Spectacle-Commodity Society" in *Situationist International Anthology*, ed. and trans. Ken Knabb. Berkeley: Bureau of Public Secrets, 1981. 157. Published under Debord's name as *Le déclin et la chute de l'économie spectaculaire-marchande*. Paris: Jean-Jacques Pauvert aux Belles Lettres, 1993. 26.

Dino, Desi and Billy. "Like a Rolling Stone," from *I'm a Fool* (Reprise, 1965).

Dion and the Belmonts. "I Wonder Why" (Laurie, 1958).

Dominoes. *The Dominoes Featuring Clyde McPhatter: 18 Hits* (King, 1996).

Don't Look Back. Directed by D. A. Pennebaker. Leacock-Pennebaker, 1967.

The Dreamers. Directed by Bernardo Bertolucci. Fox Searchlight, 2004.

Drifters. "Money Honey" (Atlantic, 1953). See Clyde McPhatter.

———"There Goes My Baby" (Atlantic, 1959). Included on *1959–1965: All-Time Greatest Hits and More* (Atlantic, 1988).

Geldof, Bob. "Turn the Bleedin' Noise Down, Bobbo." *Uncut Legends #1: Dylan*, 2003. 23.

"The Ghost of Electricity," radio documentary on Bob Dylan in Manchester, UK, 17 May 1966 (BBC, 29 June 1999). Produced and narrated by Andy Kershaw. Courtesy C. P. Lee.

Ginsberg, Allen. "A Western Ballad" (1948). See Ginsberg, *Selected Poems, 1947–1995*. New York: HarperCollins, 1996. 6–7 (with score).

Gross, Terry. Interview with Richard Belzer. *Fresh Air* (WHYY-FM, Philadelphia/NPR, 31 December 1987). Included on *Fresh Air Laughs with Terry Gross* (WHYY/NPR, 2003). Courtesy Terry Gross.

Harris, Richard. "MacArthur Park" (Dunhill, 1968).

Henderson, David. *Jimi Hendrix: Voodoo Child of the Aquarian Age*. Garden City, NY: Doubleday, 1978. 167–70.

Hendrix, Jimi. "Like a Rolling Stone." On the anthology *Monterey International Pop Festival* (Rhino, 1992). Recorded 18 June 1967.

———"Star Spangled Banner." On Hendrix, *Live at Woodstock* (MCA, 1999). Recorded 19 August 1969. With Billy Cox, bass, Mitch Mitchell, drums, Juma Sultan, percussion, Larry Lee, rhythm guitar, Jerry Velez, percussion.

————"Voodoo Chile," from *Electric Ladyland* (Reprise, 1968). As well as a faraway version of "Like a Rolling Stone," "Voodoo Chile" is a cousin to "Catfish Blues" (Robert Petway's 1940 recording is probably the first under that title, but as a commonplace theme it's decades older; Hendrix's straight recording of "Catfish Blues," from 1967, is on *Jimi Hendrix: Blues*, MCA, 1994). "Catfish Blues" is a precursor of Muddy Waters's "Rollin' Stone," which is to say a precursor of . . .

Hentoff, Nat. "The Playboy Interview: Bob Dylan." *Playboy*, March 1966. In McGregor. "That's always been the easy way" (133). "I was singing" (129).

Hilburn, Robert. "Rock's Enigmatic Poet Opens a Long-Private Door." *Los Angeles Times*, 4 April 2004.

Hitchcock, Robyn. "Like a Rolling Stone," from *Robyn Sings* (editions PAF! 2002).

The Hitmakers (segment of the series *Pop Goes the Music*). Written and directed by Morgan Neville. A & E, 27 August 2001. Available as part of the 2-DVD set *The Songmakers Collection* (A & E, 2001).

Horstman, Dorothy. *Sing Your Heart Out, Country Boy*. New York: Dutton, 1975. 323.

House, Son. "My Black Mama Part I and Part II" (Vocalion, 1930). Collected on *Son House and the Great Delta Blues Singers: Complete Recorded Works in Chronological Order, 1928–1930* (Document, 1990), which also includes Garfield Akers's "Cottonfield Blues Part I and Part II"; in 1962, both could be found on *Really! The Country Blues* (Origin Jazz Library). House rerecorded "Part II" as "Death Letter Blues" in 1965; see House, *Father of the Delta Blues: The Complete 1965 Sessions* (Columbia, 1992). "Death Letter" was covered in 2000 by the White Stripes, in 2002 by David Johansen and the Harry Smiths, and by John Mellencamp in 2003—differently and convincingly every time. Seventy years after it was first recorded the song was lingua franca, and a new kind of pop hit—a death letter that took the form of a chain letter.

Johnson, Robert. *The Complete Recordings* (Columbia, 1990) is the basic collection, but the reissues of *King of the Delta Blues Singers* (Columbia, 1998, originally issued 1961) and *King of the Delta Blues Singers, Volume II* (Columbia 2005, originally issued 1970) are more listenable. "I thought about Johnson a lot, wondered who his audience could have been," Dylan wrote in 2004 in *Chronicles, Volume One* (New York: Simon & Schuster), speaking of hearing *King of the Delta Blues Singers* before its official release. "It's hard to imagine sharecroppers or plantation field hands at hop joints, relating to songs like these. You have to wonder if Johnson was playing for an audience that only he could see, one off in the future."

Johnston, Bob, aka Colonel Jubilation B. Johnston. *Moldy Goldies: Colonel Jubilation B. Johnston and His Mystic Knights Band and Street Singers Attack the Hits* (Columbia, 1966). An album Johnston made with the Nashville component of the *Blonde on Blonde* band, locked in the studio in Nashville at four in the morning, with only a couple of hours to go before the alcohol runs out, turning the Righteous Brothers' "(You're My) Soul and Inspiration" into "Rainy Day Women #12 & 35." Turning the Mamas and the Papas' "Monday, Monday" into "Rainy Day Women #12 & 35." Turning Sonny and Cher's "Bang Bang," Shirley Ellis's "The Name Game," the Young Rascals' "Good Lovin'," the Lovin' Spoonful's "Daydream," and the McCoys' "Hang on Sloopy" into "Rainy Day Women #12 & 35." And turning Johnny Rivers's immortal "Secret Agent Man" into the even more immortal "Columbia, Gem of the Ocean." In the 1980s postmodernists croaked incessantly about pop culture and subversion; *Moldy Goldies* is an early proof of the theory lined out by the singer David Thomas in the course of a long story about how for years he heard Tammy Wynette's "Stand by Your Man" as "Stand by, Earthman": "The song had nothing to do with a global perspective, aliens, or outer space. It seemed to be a standard man-

Works Cited 251

woman tragedy—but it got to the chorus, and it was '*Stand by,*
earthman.' I couldn't believe it. The rest of us were wasting our time
with Captain Beefheart, Velvet Underground, all that stuff, while
these hillbillies, doing country music, had done *post-modern* before
the rest of us had even gotten to *neo-classical* modern. My mind—
cracked." See "Surfer Girl" on *Meadville*, in the 5-CD Thomas set
Monster (Cooking Vinyl, 1997).
———Interview with GM, 11 May 2004.
Jones, Mickey. See "The Ghost of Electricity."

Kerouac, Jack. Narration in *Pull My Daisy*. Directed by Robert Frank
and Alfred Leslie. G-String Productions, 1959.
Kooper, Al. *Backstage Passes & Backstabbing Bastards: Memoirs of a Rock 'n'
Roll Survivor*. New York: Billboard, 1998. 7.
———Interview with GM, 14 May 2004.
———"This Diamond Ring" (United Artists, 1976). Included on
Kooper, *Rare and Well Done* (Sony, 2001).

Landau, Jon. "Bob Dylan: John Wesley Harding," *Crawdaddy*, May
1968. Collected in Landau, *It's Too Late to Stop Now: A Rock and Roll
Journal*. San Francisco: Straight Arrow, 1972. 49. See McGregor,
256.
Led Zeppelin. "Stairway to Heaven," from *ZoSo* (aka "Led Zeppelin
IV") (Atlantic, 1971).
Lee, C. P. *like the night: Bob Dylan and the road to the Manchester Free Trade
Hall*. London: Helter Skelter, 1998. 155.
Lewis, Gary, and the Playboys. "This Diamond Ring" (Liberty, 1965).
Beginning as an ice-cream band at Disneyland, between January
1965 and May 1966 the group had seven consecutive Top Ten hits.
"Why do you think rock 'n' roll has become such an international
phenomenon?" Nat Hentoff asked Bob Dylan in 1966. "I can't

really think that there is any rock 'n' roll," Dylan said. "Actually, when you think about it, anything that has no real existence is bound to become an international phenomenon. Anyway, what does it mean, rock 'n' roll? Does it mean Beatles, does it mean John Lee Hooker, Bobby Vinton, Jerry Lewis' kid? What about Lawrence Welk? He must play a few rock 'n' roll songs. Are all these people really the same? Is Ricky Nelson like Otis Redding? Is Mick Jagger really Ma Rainey?" What's so remarkable about Dylan's words is the way they speak for a time when all these people could be heard as rock 'n' roll, when the term suggested not boundaries to cross, but their utter irrelevance. See McGregor, 128.

Lewis, Noah (aka Noah Lewis Jug Band). "New Minglewood Blues" (Victor, 1930). A follow-up to Gus Cannon and His Jug Stompers' 1928 "Minglewood Blues," with Lewis on harmonica, "New Minglewood Blues" can be found on the anthology *Blues: 36 Masterpieces of Blues Music* (Frémeaux & Associés, 1995) and many other collections.

Little Richard. "Ready Teddy" (Specialty, 1956).

Marsh, Dave. *The Heart of Rock & Soul: The 1001 Greatest Singles Ever Made* (1989). New York: Da Capo, 1999. Marvin Gaye's "I Heard It Through the Grapevine" is number one.

Masked and Anonymous. Directed by Larry Charles, written by Sergei Petrov and Rene Fontaine (pseud. Larry Charles and Bob Dylan). Sony Pictures Classics, 2003.

Masked and Anonymous: Music from the Motion Picture (Columbia, 2003).

McGuire, Barry. "Eve of Destruction" (Dunhill, 1965). As *Golden Protest* unfortunately remains unissued, McGuire's still-shameless, still-growly, still-stirring hit has to be heard on collections on the order of the 8-CD box set *The Folk Years* (Time-Life, 2002), which, golden protest–wise, also includes the Byrds' version of "The

Times They Are A-Changin'," Trini Lopez's "If I Had a Hammer," Janis Ian's "Society's Child," Glen Campbell's version of "Universal Soldier," Dion's "Abraham, Martin and John," and the Kingston Trio's version of "Blowin' in the Wind."

McNamara, Robert. "Going to hell." In Taylor Branch, *Pillar of Fire: America in the King Years, 1963–65.* New York: Simon and Schuster, 1998. 543.

McPhatter, Clyde. McPhatter's unmatched 1953–54 recordings with the Drifters (along with "Money Honey," "The Way I Feel," "Let the Boogie Woogie Roll"—try and stop it—"Such a Night," "Bip Bam," "What'cha Gonna Do," "Honey Love," "White Christmas," and "The Bells of St. Mary's") can be found on the Drifters' *Let the Boogie Woogie Roll: Greatest Hits 1953–1958* (Atlantic, 1988) and on McPhatter's *The Forgotten Angel* (32 R&B), which also includes his later solo recordings, many of them hits ("Treasure of Love," 1956, number 16, the stately "Without Love (There Is Nothing)," 1957, number 19, "A Lover's Question," 1958, number 6, "Lover Please," 1962, number 7, plus three songs recorded live at the Apollo Theater in 1964. See also Dominoes. Jesse Stone, the composer of "Money Honey," died 1 April 1999, at the age of ninety-nine; perhaps in tribute, later that year Dylan essayed a trail-dragging version of the song to a crowd in Ithaca, New York. Included on *The Genuine Never-Ending Tour: The Covers Collection 1988-2000* (Wild Wolf bootleg).

Mellers, Wilfred. *A Darker Shade of Pale: A Backdrop to Bob Dylan.* New York: Oxford University Press, 1985. 140.

Metcalfe, Malcolm. See "The Ghost of Electricity."

Mosley, Walter. *Little Scarlet.* New York: Little, Brown, 2004. 218, 17, 78. When Mosley began his series of Easy Rawlins murder mysteries in 1990, with *Devil in a Blue Dress*, the setting was 1948, but in the way Mosley dramatized the special atmosphere of racism in postwar Los Angeles, the specter of the Watts riots was already present. The novels that followed—*A Red Death* (1991, set in 1953), *White Butterfly* (1992, set in 1956), *Black Betty* (1994, set in 1961), *A Little Yellow Dog* (1996, set in 1963), and *Bad Boy Brawly Brown* (2003, set in early 1964)—traced the social history of the city from the perspective of a black man who had learned to trust absolutely nothing about it, but they also seemed like a holding action, as if the closer Mosley came to the riots, to the inevitable, perhaps even uncrossable divide in his tale and his hero's times, the more terrifying the riots became. Set in 1965, just after the riots, *Little Scarlet* crossed the gap. It dove deeper than the books before it, and set a new stage.

Muldaur, Geoff. "Got to Find Blind Lemon, Part One," on *The Secret Handshake* (Hightone, 1998) and "Got to Find Blind Lemon, Part Two," on *Password* (Hightone, 2000).

Murray, Charles Shaar. *Crosstown Traffic*. New York: St. Martin's, 1989. 63.

Mystery Tramps. "Like a Rolling Stone" ("30th St. Mix vocal," "30th St. Mix instrumental," "Radio Mix," "1–800 Mix") (Imago, 1993). Courtesy Dave Marsh.

National Lampoon. *Radio Dinner* (Banana/Blue Thumb, 1972). Including, along with "Those Fabulous Sixties," horrifyingly funny attacks on John Lennon, Yoko Ono, Joan Baez, and George Harrison's 1971 Concert for Bangladesh.

Nelson, Paul. "Bob Dylan," in *The Rolling Stone Illustrated History of Rock & Roll*, ed. Jim Miller. New York: Rolling Stone/Random House, 1976. 208. Replaced in later editions of the book, unfortunately; certainly the most idiosyncratic and, aside from Dylan's 2002 stage announcement, probably the least pretentious overview of Dylan's career there is.

———"Newport Folk Festival, 1965." *Sing Out!* September 1965. In McGregor, 73.

Paul Butterfield Blues Band. *An Anthology: The Elektra Years* (Elektra, 1997). Includes Mike Bloomfield's first recordings, from 1965, notably his hot-shot solo on "Nut Popper #1" and his fierce between-the-lines work on "Born in Chicago," the latter from *The Paul Butterfield Blues Band*, plus his nothing-to-prove solo on Robert Johnson's "Walking Blues" from the Butterfield band's 1966 *East-West*.

Pet Shop Boys. "Go West." From *Very* (EMI/ERG, 1993). Five additional mixes (including "Farley & Heller Fire Island Mix," which would seem to defeat the concept) are on the dispensable "Go West" (EMI/ERG, 1993).

Phillips, John. Notes to *Monterey International Pop Festival* (Rhino, 1992).

Pisaro, Michael. Letter to GM, 28 March 2004.

Poston, Shirley. "We Had Known a Lion." KRLA's *The Beat*, 2 October 1965. Reprinted as liner insert to Dylan, *We Had Known a Lion*.

Presley, Elvis. "Can't Help Falling in Love" (RCA, 1961).

——"Mystery Train" (Sun, 1955).

Radice, Paula. Radice's unique account of hearing "Like a Rolling Stone" for the first time was included on the BBC Radio 4 documentary "Soul Music—Programme 5: Like a Rolling Stone" (BBC Birmingham, 27 July 2004, produced by Lindsay Leonard). Radice contributes regularly to the Internet Dylan magazine *freewheelin-on-line*.

Replacements. "Like a Rolling Pin" (1990). Included on *All for Nothing/Nothing for All* (1997).

Ridgway, Stan. "Classic Hollywood Ending," from *Snakebite: Blacktop Ballads & Fugitive Songs* (redFLY, 2004).

Righteous Brothers. "You've Lost that Lovin' Feeling" (Philles, 1964).

Rolling Stones. "Like a Rolling Stone," from *Stripped* (Virgin, 1995). They start from the top, and immediately wipe the floor with countless other attempts, including many of Dylan's own. Mick Jagger sings in a country voice—he makes you turn up the volume to hear him, and his shouts of "Yeah!" at the beginning of each verse are an acknowledgment that the listener knows this song as well or better than he does. Dylan's onstage duet with Jagger, from Montpellier, France, on 27 July 1995, is collected on the Dylan bootleg *I've Got a Song to Sing: A Compilation of Rare Performances in 1996* (no label).

Rozanov, Vasily. "No more coats." Quoted in Raoul Vaneigem, *Traité de savoir-vivre à l'usage des jeunes générations*. Paris: Gallimard, 1967. 180–81. As *The Revolution of Everyday Life*, trans. Donald Nicholson-Smith, London: Rebel Press, and Seattle: Left Bank Books, 1994. 176.

Shelton, Robert. *No Direction Home*. New York: Beech Tree, 1986. 279.

Spector, Phil. "Phil Spector: The Rolling Stone Interview" (Jann Wenner). *Rolling Stone*, 1 November 1969. Collected in *The Rolling Stone Interviews, 1967–1980*. New York: Rolling Stone/St. Martin's, 1981. 63.

Spitz, Bob. *Dylan: A Biography*. New York: McGraw-Hill, 1989. 299.

Springsteen, Bruce. "The Rock and Roll Hall of Fame Speech" (1988). Collected in *Studio A: The Bob Dylan Reader*, ed. Benjamin Hedin. New York: W.W. Norton, 2004. 202.

Stanley Brothers. "Little Maggie" (Rich-R-Tone, 1948). On *Earliest Recordings* (Revenant, 1997).

Stewart, Rod. "Rod Stewart: The Rolling Stone Interview" (John Morthland). *Rolling Stone*, 24 December 1970. Collected in *The Rolling Stone Interviews, 1967–1980*. New York: Rolling Stone/St. Martin's, 1981. 121. Stewart once said that if he ever sang "A Change Is Gonna Come," that would mean he was quitting forever, because he could never again face the public after failing to live up to that song, which he has always wanted to sing. So far he's kept his promise, but his 1973 version of "Twistin' the Night Away" lives up to Cooke's 1962 original.

Stone, Allen. Interview with Bob Dylan. WDTM, Detroit, 24 October 1965. Included on *Dylan: 1965 Revisited* (Great Dane bootleg).

Tales of Rock 'N' Roll: Highway 61 Revisited. Written and directed by James Marsh (BBC/Arena, 1993). One of four such 1993 hour-long films by Marsh: the others are on Lou Reed's "Walk on the Wild Side," Elvis Presley's "Heartbreak Hotel," and Buddy Holly's "Peggy Sue," one of the most inspired of all rock 'n' roll documentaries.

Temptations. "Papa Was a Rollin' Stone" (Gordy, 1972).

Turtles. "Like a Rolling Stone," from *It Ain't Me Babe* (White Whale, 1965). Reissued on Sundazed, 1994.

USA for Africa. "We Are the World" (Columbia, 1985). For mean-spirited comment, see "Number One with a Bullet," from *Artforum*, May 1985, in my *In the Fascist Bathroom* (as *Ranters and Crowd Pleasers*, 1993), Cambridge, MA, 1999, London, Viking, 1993, and as *Im Faschistischen Badezimmer*, Hamburg, Germany: Rogner & Bernhard, 1994.

Valens, Ritchie. "La Bamba"/"Donna" (Del-Fi, 1958).

Wailers. "Rolling Stone" (Studio One, 1966). Included on Bob Marley and the Wailers' *One Love at Studio One* (Heartbeat, 1991).

Waters, Muddy. "Rollin' Stone" (Aristocrat, 1950).

Wenner, Jann. Interview with GM, 11 May 2004.

———"A Letter from the Editor," *Rolling Stone*, 9 November 1967.

Wesdon, John. "Highway 61" (1993). Featured in James Marsh's *Tales of Rock 'N' Roll: Highway 61 Revisited*.

Williams, Hank. "Lost Highway." (MGM, 1949).

Williamson, Sonny Boy (aka Rice Miller). "Don't Start Me Talkin'" (Checker, 1955). Included on *His Best* (Chess/MCA, 1997).

Young Rascals. "Like a Rolling Stone," from *The Young Rascals* (Atlantic, 1966)

Zappa, Frank. In Clinton Heylin. *Dylan: Behind the Shades—The Biography, Take Two* (London: Viking, 2000). 205.

Acknowledgments

Since it was his idea, it can be said without hyperbole that this book would not exist without Clive Priddle of PublicAffairs. Working with him has been a continuing pleasure, as it has with publisher Peter Osnos, design director Nina D'Amario and designer Mark McGarry, managing editor Robert Kimzey, sales director Matty Goldberg, publicist Jaime Leifer, and publicity director Gene Taft; copy editor John Guardiano and indexer Robert Swanson both did a wonderful job. At Faber & Faber, as I have for many years I owe much to Jon Riley, and also to Lee Brackstone, Angus Cargill, and Helen Francis. At Kiepenheuer & Witsch, I have benefited from the enthusiasm and professionalism of Birgit Schmitz and, far too often for comfort, the bottomless knowledge, limitless patience, and indefatigable error-catching of translator Fritz Schneider. Wendy Weil and Emily Forland of the

Wendy Weil Agency made me feel lucky, as always, as did Anthony Goff of the David Higham Agency in London and Christian Dittus and Peter Fritz of the Paul and Peter Fritz Agency in Zurich.

There are others whose aid and comfort were indispensable. In his laconically amused way, Jeff Rosen of Special Rider Music made the trickiest problems seem like the simplest; in his office, Diane Lapson, Lynne Okin, and Robert Bower were instantly helpful and always friendly. In the course of easy conversations and a letter, Jann Wenner, Al Kooper, Bob Johnston, and Michael Pisaro gave me more than they could have had any way of knowing, and I exploited what they gave me to the full. Whenever there was a Dylan performance I had to hear, Kevin Reilly immediately knew where it was—and with intimations of unimagined treasures to come. When I chanced on Mick Brownfield's comic strip, I knew he had caught the subject of this book in a way I never could, and I thank him for just saying yes when I asked if I could find a way to put his version of "Like a Rolling Stone" along side of mine. I could not have worked without the warm and enthusiastic support of Sony Legacy; Jeff Jones, John Jackson, Tom Cording, and especially Steve Berkowitz provided invaluable help with recordings and photographs. Sean Wilentz discovered both main title and subtitle one September morning in the back of a New York taxicab.

I owe a special debt to those people and institutions that over the years gave me a chance to try out some of the themes and some of the words that found their way into these pages: Bill Strachan of Henry Holt, the Dorothy and Lillian Gish Foundation, Joe Levy at *Rolling Stone*, the Centre Georges Pompidou in Paris, Michel Braudeau of *La Nouvelle Revue Française* and translator Julia Dorner, John Harris and the J. Paul Getty Museum, Robert Hull of Time-Life Music, Perry Richardson of A Publishing, Steve Wasserman of the *Los Angeles Times Book Review*, Ingrid Sischy, Graham Fuller, Scott Cohen and Brad Goldfarb at *Interview*, Jack Bankowsky, David Frankel, and Sydney Pokorny at *Artforum*, Bill Wyman at *Salon*, Wendy Lesser at *Threepenny Review*, Lindsay Leonard and Sarah Howell of BBC Birmingham, and Melissa Maerz and Steve Perry at *City Pages* in Minneapolis.

Other people helped me with ideas, records, archival photographs, old letters, rare publications, expertise, breaking news, a glad hand and simple presence: Liz Bordow, Sue D'Alonzo, Glen Dundas, Barry Franklin, Mike Gordon, Terry Gross of *Fresh Air*, Andy Kershaw, C. P. Lee, Bill Marcus, Cecily Marcus, Emily Marcus, David Gans of Truth and Fun, B. George of the ARChive of Contemporary Music, Dave Marsh, Paula Radice, Mary Rome, Bob Steiner, Patrick Thomas, Steve Weinstein, Greg Tomeoni of Copy Central in Berkeley, Eric Weisbard of the Experience Music Project in Seattle, David Vest, Sara Bernstein, and especially Steve Mack.

As Jenny Marcus said when Clive Priddle first called, in one way or another I've been writing this book for as long as

"Like a Rolling Stone" has been on the air. We heard Bob Dylan sing it at the Berkeley Community Theater in December 1965, at the Grand in San Francisco in October 2004, and many times gratifying and dispiriting, predictable and surprising, in between. All that time.

Index

264 *Index*

Baez, Joan (*cont.*)
Dylan and, 16–17, 56, 120, 179
at Newport, 153
recordings of, 244
Baez, Mimi, 14, 15
"Ball and Chain" (Big Brother and the Holding Company), 108
The Ballad of Ramblin' Jack—Original Soundtrack (Elliott), 230
"Ballad of a Thin Man" (Dylan), 112, 142, 169, 182
The Band, 26, 160, 161n, 188, 191, 231, 237
Barker, Derek, 229
Barry, Jeff, 137
Basement Tapes (Dylan), 166n
"Be My Baby" (Ronettes), 140
The Beach Boys, 44
The Beat (KRLA), 135, 161–62, 179, 235, 255
The Beatles
in America, 56
on charts, xi, 4, 5, 6, 43, 44
drum intros, 95n
Dylan and, 61, 145
early ambition of, 3
Ed Sullivan show, 155
Before the Flood (Dylan), 191
Bell, Madelaine, 190
Belzer, Richard, 148–49, 150, 151, 244, 248
Bennett, Tony, 54

Bennett, Will, 123, 244
The Bently Boys, 62
Berlin, Irving, 100
Bernstein, Sara, 238, 239
Berry, Chuck, 60, 61–62, 99, 107, 166n, 183, 244
Bertolucci, Bernardo, 170, 248
The Best of Bob Dylan, volume 2, 230, 232
Best, Pete, 135
Big Brother and the Holding Company, 108
Biograph (Dylan), 232, 241
The Black Labels, 187, 244
"Blind Willie McTell" (Dylan), 26, 230
Blonde on Blonde (Dylan), 136, 142, 172, 187, 205, 230, 241, 259
Blood on the Tracks (Dylan), 191–95, 230
Bloomfield, Michael
with Butterfield, 254
career of, 107–9
on Dylan, 109–10, 244
with Dylan live, 130, 131, 187
Dylan on, 106–7
on Johnson, Robert, 131
Kooper on, 110–11
at "Like a Rolling Stone" sessions, xi, 116, 117–18, 126, 203, 205–14, 216, 217, 219–22, 234
at Newport, 154–55, 158
on "Tombstone Blues," 168

Hajdu, David, 60, 156
Halee, Roy, xi
Hamilton, Richard, 61–62
Hammond, John, 139, 140,
    141n, 142n
"Handsome Molly" (Dylan), 25,
    231
Hannan, Patrick, 188
"A Hard Rain's A-Gonna Fall"
    (Dylan), 56–57, 122, 161,
    231
Harris, Ed, 75
Harris, Emmylou, 186
Harris, Regina, 189
Harris, Richard, 189, 248
Harrison, George, 34n, 254
Hawkins, Dale, 107
The Hawks, 26, 51, 56, 160,
    165n, 177, 179, 180–81,
    183, 188, 235, 236, 241
*The Heart of Rock & Soul: The 1001
    Greatest Singles Ever Made*
    (Marsh), 252
"Heartbreak Hotel" (Presley),
    224, 257
Hedin, Benjamin, 256
"Hellhound on My Trail" (John-
    son), 103
Helm, Levon, 160, 178, 241
"Help" (Beatles), xi
Henderson, David, 89–91,
    249
Hendrix, Jimi, 77–78, 89–91,

101, 108, 170, 182, 190,
    248–49
Hentoff, Nat, 33, 55, 242, 249,
    251
Herman's Hermits, 43, 44
"He's Sure the Boy I Love" (Crys-
    tals), 140
"Hey Little Richard" (Dylan),
    156, 231, 232
Heylin, Clinton, 258
"High Lonesome Hill" (Curtis),
    27, 247
"Highlands" (Dylan), 26, 195,
    199–200, 201, 232
"Highway 61" (Wesdon), 257
Highway 61 Interactive (Dylan),
    232, 234
Highway 61 Revisited (Dylan), 232,
    240
  as best rock 'n' roll album, 190
  highway lore and, 167
  imitations of, 147n
  Johnston and, 136, 142, 143
  as map, 104, 153, 163, 168,
    173, 175, 200
  at Newport, 155
  opening of, 94
  sessions for, 144, 159
  songs on, 112, 161, 172
"Highway 61 Revisited" (Dylan),
    170, 191
Hilburn, Robert, 185, 249
Hill, Walter, 186

PublicAffairs is a publishing house founded in 1997. It is a tribute to the standards, values, and flair of three persons who have served as mentors to countless reporters, writers, editors, and book people of all kinds, including me.

I. F. STONE, proprietor of *I. F. Stone's Weekly*, combined a commitment to the First Amendment with entrepreneurial zeal and reporting skill and became one of the great independent journalists in American history. At the age of eighty, Izzy published *The Trial of Socrates*, which was a national bestseller. He wrote the book after he taught himself ancient Greek.

BENJAMIN C. BRADLEE was for nearly thirty years the charismatic editorial leader of *The Washington Post*. It was Ben who gave the *Post* the range and courage to pursue such historic issues as Watergate. He supported his reporters with a tenacity that made them fearless and it is no accident that so many became authors of influential, best-selling books.

ROBERT L. BERNSTEIN, the chief executive of Random House for more than a quarter century, guided one of the nation's premier publishing houses. Bob was personally responsible for many books of political dissent and argument that challenged tyranny around the globe. He is also the founder and longtime chair of Human Rights Watch, one of the most respected human rights organizations in the world.

For fifty years, the banner of Public Affairs Press was carried by its owner, Morris B. Schnapper, who published Gandhi, Nasser, Toynbee, Truman, and about 1,500 other authors. In 1983, Schnapper was described by *The Washington Post* as "a redoubtable gadfly." His legacy will endure in the books to come.

Peter Osnos, *Publisher*